Spring Boot 2

How To Get Started and Build a Microservice

third edition

Jens Boje

CODEBOJE

Brief books for developers

Spring Boot 2
Jens Boje

third edition

ISBN: 9781694462831

rev. 3.0

Published in 2019 by Jens Boje

Jens Boje
Pfungststr. 3
60314 Frankfurt
Germany

On the web: *http://codeboje.de*
Please send errors to *book@codeboje.de*

Publisher: Jens Boje

Contents

README

Learning to build applications and especially APIs with Spring and Spring Boot is exciting. At the same time, it is freighting when you stay at the bottom of Mt. Spring.

Spring Boot makes it much easier than it was with Spring alone in the past. However, it also hides much of the complexity involved in its magic, which brings in new complexity and might leave you confused sometimes.

Be assured that this is totally normal and everyone went through this phase. When you hike up, it gets easier as you will gain a solid understanding and control of the complexity involved and you can build frictionless applications with it.

I know I felt this way when I first started out with Spring, and there was no Spring Boot at that time. But, that's temporary, and it gets much better over time. When I walked up Mt. Spring a bit, it already got easier. And it wasn't just me, I noticed the same with friends and co-workers.

In the book, I reduce the complexity and focus on small, manageable parts, so you get productive quickly. It is the same approach I use successfully in my workshops or when helping co-workers in-person. Unlike in-person interaction, I'm not with you to see you when you progress through the book. Therefore, I can't notice when you have a question so I can rephrase and explain it differently. Nonetheless, you are not alone, you can ask me, and I will help you get unstuck. Promise– just email me.

Introduction

This book's approach differs from that of other programming books that you may have encountered. I believe that the best way to learn a new framework or language is to build applications using it. I also assume that you have some experience with Java, Maven, and the IDE of your choice.

The application for the book is modeled after a real production application serving thousands of requests and running smoothly since its first deployment. The sample application follows the same implementation approach but leaves out certain complexities which are not needed for learning to build a microservice with Spring Boot.

The original application stores binary files and certain metadata, like product references, width, and height of images, file size, for covers and other marketing materials of books. The application is integrated into a large infrastructure and offers all of its services GUI-less. However, for the sample application, we will do something simpler for learning and are going to develop a commenting system.

What will the application do:

- store comments for products or pages

- check comments for spam and flag them accordingly

- provide a restful interface to add, delete and retrieve the comments

What we will build in this book:

- a simple SpamDetector for learning to use Spring Core

- a persistence tier using Spring Data JPA

- a service Layer using our previously build storage and integrating our SpamDetector module for spam detection

- a RESTful API using Spring MVC

We will test our microservice, make it production-ready with Spring Boots' features, and finally deploy it as a standalone microservice.

The full source code of this book's sample application is available on GitHub: https://github.com/azarai/springbootbook-3rd-edition

The project uses a Multi Module Maven layout. Build and run instructions are in the repository.

I also added all external reference to a private resource page for your convenience: http://codeboje.de/sbb-resources

If you have any questions, do not hesitate to contact me at the email address found in the last chapter.

You Don't Need a Specific IDE

I wrote the book intentionally without using a particular IDE in mind for various reasons.

1. You can build Spring Boot applications with any IDE or with plain Texteditor and Maven

2. I might not use your loved IDE and thus either force you to use an IDE you do not know or like, which is terrible for learning. You don't want to learn two things at a time.

3. Screenshots of IDEs are pretty fast outdated anyways.

4. Use the IDE you are comfortable with because you only have to learn one new thing, Spring Boot.

Honestly, fighting with an IDE and learning a new tech at the same time is a waste of your time. Learn one after another and when you start with Spring Boot now, use an IDE you are familiar with.

What You Will Need

- Java 8+

- Maven (3.2+) or optionally Gradle (see note below)

- IDE or Texteditor of your choice (the book is written IDE independent, but I use STS personally)

Installing and setting them up is not in the scope of this book.

You can use Gradle instead of Maven, but the book and the examples assume you are using Maven. However, I assume you are capable of converting it to Gradle yourself.

If you are new to Maven, check out the brief introduction to Maven in Appendix A. It will assist you in following along.

Understanding Spring Core

In the first chapter, we will take a closer look at the Spring Framework and what kind of problems it solves in the first place. We then examine how the core of it works and how to use it. We will focus on the basics here and ignore the numerous features it offers additionally; some of them will be covered further in the book.

If you already know what the Spring Core does and how it works, you can skip to the next chapter and directly start with Spring Boot.

We are using Maven as a build and dependency management tool in the book. If you are new to Maven, check out the brief introduction to Maven in Appendix A; it covers the basic to get started. And if you want to use Gradle, go ahead and use it, I assume you are capable of converting the dependencies to Gradle yourself.

What is the Spring Framework?

The Spring Framework provides an environment for developing Java applications so you can focus on developing your application logic. Standard functionality and inter-component connectivity are taken care of by Spring, and you save time in each project as you do not have to reinvent the wheels each time.

Spring uses the concept of Inversion of Control (IoC). IoC means that service calls are not hardwired but instead run through a framework, i.e., service A uses service B but does not know how B is instantiated - the IoC container does it.

This concept gives us some benefits like:

* decoupling service calls from the actual implementation of the task

* makes it easier to change an implementation of a service

- our application gets more modular, and we can switch parts without rewriting lots of services

- decoupled services also mean we can test each individual service better without real dependencies; we can mock them

IoC can be implemented in various patterns like Factory, service locators, or with Dependency Injection (DI). Spring uses the latter, DI.

DI frees your services from knowing how to instantiate and connect other services (yours or foreign). Spring handles it at startup of the application.

It is best understood by seeing it in action. So let's step back for now and start with a simple example of service coupling traditionally. For that, we create a simple spam checking command-line application.

You can find the full source code of this chapter in the spring-core-exercise directory of the GitHub repository. It is a working sample, and you use it as a reference at any time.

We will use the service later, so let's create a new Maven project by creating a pom.xml like:

```xml
<project
  xmlns="http://maven.apache.org/POM/4.0.0"
  xmlns:xsi="http://www.w3.org/2001/XMLSchema-instance"
  xsi:schemaLocation="http://maven.apache.org/POM/4.0.0
   http://maven.apache.org/xsd/maven-4.0.0.xsd">
  <modelVersion>4.0.0</modelVersion>

  <groupId>de.codeboje.springbootbook</groupId>
  <artifactId>spam-detection</artifactId>
  <version>1.0.0-SNAPSHOT</version>

  <!-- Project metadata -->
  <name>Spring Boot Book - Spam Detection</name>

  <dependencies>
    <dependency>
      <groupId>junit</groupId>
      <artifactId>junit</artifactId>
```

```
        <version>4.12</version>
        <scope>test</scope>
      </dependency>
    </dependencies>
  </project>
```

Next, we create a simple *SimpleSpamDetector*, which checks a given string if it contains one of our predefined spam words.

```
public class SimpleSpamDetector {

    private List<String> spamWords = new ArrayList<String>();

    public SimpleSpamDetector( List<String> spamWords) {
        this.spamWords = spamWords;
    }

    public boolean containsSpam( String value) {
        for (String spam : spamWords) {
            if (value.toLowerCase().contains(spam)) {
                return true;
            }
        }
        return false;
    }
}
```

Now, let's create an application for it. The application takes the first command line argument and checks it for spam. In the early version, we will hard code the spam words like:

```
public class SpamCheckerApplication {

    public static void main(String[] args) {

        List<String> spamWords = new ArrayList<String>();
        spamWords.add("viagra");

        SimpleSpamDetector spamDetector = new SimpleSpamDetector(spamWords);
        System.out.println( spamDetector.containsSpam(args[0]) );
```

```
        }
    }
```

For simplicity, we print the result to the console.

Run the application now and verify that it detects viagra as a spam word in a text.

Hardcoded spam words are pretty senseless, don't you think? So the next logical step would be to put the spam words in a file, so let's do it in the main method. We also retrieve the filename as a second command line parameter:

```
public static void main(String[] args) throws Exception {
    List<String> spamWords = new ArrayList<String>();

    if (args.length == 2) {
        spamWords = Files.readAllLines( Paths.get(args[1]) );
    }

    SimpleSpamDetector spamDetector = new SimpleSpamDetector(spamWords);
    System.out.println( spamDetector.containsSpam(args[0]) );
}
```

If we do not pass the filename as the second argument, we run with an empty spam word list. Now we will create a file for the spam words and put a few each on a single line. Run it and verify it is working before we continue.

The main method contains our control flow and the initialization of our application and its components. Usually, you would separate them, so it is a bit more maintainable. However, in this approach either our service, i.e., *SimpleSpamDetector* would be passed into the control flow or its dependencies, the spam words and filename must be passed along so the control flow or any other services using the *SimpleSpamDetector* can create its own instance. (Figure 1)

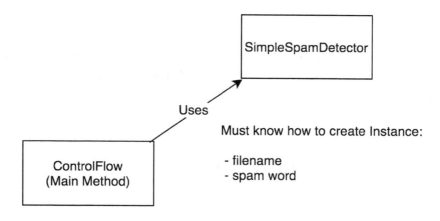

Figure 1: SpamDetector with Main Class

In the first variation, we will have a considerable center part for setting up and wiring components. With the second variation, we reduce the center lump but scatter the setup around the components.

It works in a simple example like this, but now imagine the checker is much more complex. For example, reading from multiple input sources, using different spam detectors and logic what to do when it is spam (Figure 2).

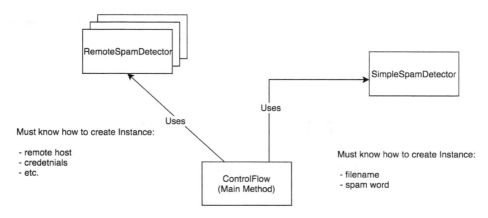

Figure 2: Illustration the problem with multiple SpamDetectors

When your application grows, and you keep it like above, it will eventually become a maintenance nightmare. However, there are solutions for this, even without Spring, and we will examine one in the next section.

A Solution Without Spring

In this section, we are going to add a second spam detector and introduce a better setup using the Factory pattern.

The Factory pattern is a standard software development pattern and helps in creating objects without knowing the exact implementation which will be created and how it is created. (Figure 3)

When working with factories and multiple implementations of a service, you will create a common interface, which each of the implementations must extend.

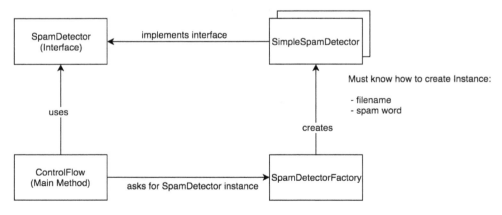

Figure 3: A solution with the Factory pattern

So, let's extract it from the *SimpleSpamDetector*. It will look like:

```java
public interface SpamDetector {

    boolean containsSpam(String value);

}
```

Next, the *SimpleSpamDetector* must extend it by:

```java
public class SimpleSpamDetector implements SpamDetector {
    // rest omitted
}
```

Now, we create the factory and move the initialization of the *SimpleSpamDetector* to it:

```java
public class SpamDetectorFactory {

    public static SpamDetector getInstance(String[] args)
    throws IOException {

        List<String> spamWords = new ArrayList<String>();

        if (args.length == 2) {
            spamWords = Files.readAllLines( Paths.get(args[1]) );
        }

        return new SimpleSpamDetector( spamWords );
    }
}
```

By using factories, you have multiple options of how to get parameters. The usual ways are:

- pass a global config object along; the main part of the application is responsible for creating it

- each factory has its own config files

- using static code blocks and hard-wired parameters

They do work, and it depends on your context which way to choose. However, we won't go deeper into these as it is not necessary to understand Spring. Nonetheless, I can tell you it 's not a good idea to mix them. I once worked on a project where all three ways were actively used in a single application. It was no fun and time consuming to find out where to configure something.

For this example, we keep it simple and just use the arguments from the main method and pass them along. It acts as a global config.

In our *SpamCheckerApplication* we will use the Factory now like:

```java
public static void main(String[] args) throws Exception {

    SpamDetector spamDetector = SpamDetectorFactory.getInstance(args);
    System.out.println( spamDetector.containsSpam(args[0]) );

}
```

In the next step, we are adding a second spam detector and assume it will do a remote check. We are not actually going to implement the check, just the base construct for showing a glimpse of the rising complexity.

```java
public class RemoteSpamDetector implements SpamDetector {

    public RemoteSpamDetector(String url, String username, String password) {
        // omitted, not needed for explanation
    }

    public boolean containsSpam(String value) {
        // make the remote call
        return false;
    }

}
```

The dummy *RemoteSpamDetector* needs three parameters to work, a URL, a username, and a password. We will create it in the *SpamDetectorFactory* as well and define, if the application retrieves more than two arguments, we should do a remote check and use the additional arguments for the *RemoteSpamDetector*.

```
public static SpamDetector getInstance( String[] args ) throws IOException {

    if (args.length <= 2) {
        List<String> spamWords = new ArrayList<String>();
        spamWords = Files.readAllLines( Paths.get(args[1]) );
        return new SimpleSpamDetector( spamWords );
    }

    return new RemoteSpamDetector( args[1], args[2], args[3] );
}
```

Remember, it looks different in a real-world application following this pattern. You wouldn't rely on command line args like that. Anyway, it is enough to grasp the concept and see where we are heading.

Imagine now, how this will end if you add more services and implementations to our application. You will have a bunch of factories and config files. If you move the initialization to the application starter now, you will be basically on your first step towards IoC. However, your services still depend on the factories and are thus always coupled to the initialization of the other services.

Of course, you can implement it in a cleaner and maintainable way. However, the main disadvantage is that you have to start all over again for your next application.

This is where Spring Core, with its Dependency Injection, rescues us. It takes over our application initialization, gets rid of the factories, and provides a runtime for loading and coupling our services. And we can use it over and over again without reinventing it each time.

In the next section, we migrate our application to Spring.

Spring Core in Action

The first thing we do in a new application is to give control of creating our services to the Spring Container. The Container initializes the services and also injects dependencies, i.e., our *SimpleSpamDetector* into the control flow.

13

A service just declares that it needs a service that implements the SpamDetector interface, and the Spring Container provides it. The only requirement now is that everything must be supervised and controlled by Spring.

In the center of Spring is the Spring Container also referred to as context or *Application-Context* (the interface). It knows every registered class and how they connect to each other.

A class made available in the context is called a bean. Beans are usually plain old Java objects (POJO) and often implement certain interfaces. In the context, each bean is identified by its id (aka name) and its type (the class). The identifier is unique across the context, and if you provide it multiple times, a previously defined one will be replaced by the new one. By default, all beans in the context are handled as singletons. You can change that, but we do not cover it in the book (search for scope and prototype).

Before we switch to Spring now, let's first move the control flow from the main method into its own class like:

```java
public class ControlFlow {

    public void run(String[] args) throws IOException {
        SpamDetector spamDetector = SpamDetectorFactory.getInstance(args);
        System.out.println( spamDetector.containsSpam(args[0]) );
    }
}
```

And the main application is reduced to:

```java
public class SpamCheckerApplication {

    public static void main(String[] args) throws Exception {
        new ControlFlow().run(args);
    }
}
```

Now, we are ready to use Spring. However, before we dive into the code, let's illustrate the concept (Figure 4) first.

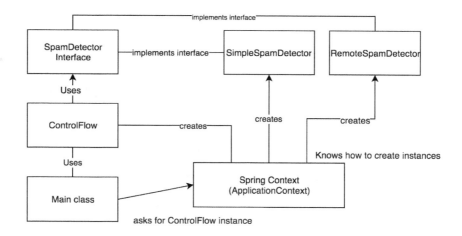

Figure 4: A solution using Spring

The Spring Context knows now how to create the instances of our *ControlFlow*, *SimpleSpamDetector*, and *RemoteSpamDetector* classes. It is created by the main class and instructed on how to detect depending class — more on that in a moment.

At first sight, it looks almost identical to the solution using the Factory pattern. However, it has some advantages, which we will cover at the end of this section. Our main class now asks the Spring Context for an instance of ControlFlow and executes the spam check on it. *ControlFlow* itself uses a *SpamDetector* but does not know or care about which type it receives. The *SpamDetector* instances and also the *ControlFlow* are Spring Beans, and under the control of Spring, so it will automatically create and connect instances.

Let's move on with the code and see in action how to create a Spring Context, how to populate and finally use it.

First, we add the dependency to our project:

```
<dependency>
  <groupId>org.springframework</groupId>
  <artifactId>spring-context</artifactId>
  <version>5.1.5.RELEASE</version>
</dependency>
```

Next, we create the context.

```java
public class SpamCheckerApplication {

    public static void main(String[] args) throws Exception {
        ApplicationContext context =
                new AnnotationConfigApplicationContext(
                        SpamAppConfig.class
                );
        context.getBean( ControlFlow.class ).run(args);
    }
}
```

The context is created by the line:

```java
ApplicationContext context = new AnnotationConfigApplicationContext(
                                SpamAppConfig.class
                    );
```

AnnotationConfigApplicationContext will start the Spring Container and load the config from a class named *SpamAppConfig*. *SpamAppConfig* is a regular POJO with a particular annotation on it, so Spring accepts it as a configuration and populates the context. More on that in a minute.

The *ApplicationContext* comes in two styles. The first one is by defining all our beans in an XML document following various Spring XML schema and the second one is to use the Java based configuration with annotations. We will use the latter as it is the norm now and will spare you some brain damage by not using XML.

To mark our *SpamAppConfig* as a configuration source, we annotate it with *@Configuration*. In it, we define our beans:

```java
@Configuration
public class SpamAppConfig {

    @Bean
    public SpamDetector simpleSpamDetector (

    @Value("${sbb.spamwords.filename}")
```

```
        String filename

    ) throws IOException {

        List<String> spamWords = new ArrayList<String>();
        spamWords = Files.readAllLines( Paths.get(filename) );
        return new SimpleSpamDetector( spamWords );
    }

    @Bean
    public ControlFlow controlFlow( SpamDetector spamDetector ) {
        return new ControlFlow( spamDetector );
    }
}
```

In a *@Configuration*, we provide the beans by adding methods creating an instance and annotate these with the *@Bean* annotation.

Those methods can have parameters, and Spring tries to resolve these by other provided beans in the context. In this case, it will expect to have one and exact one bean in the context. It is a shortcut for the *@Autowired* annotation; more on that soon. Spring will load the beans in order to resolve dependencies. It will use the method name as the bean identifier in the context, except we declare a different one with the *@Bean* annotation like:

```
@Bean("myBean")
```

Or:

```
@Bean(name="myBean")
```

For referencing the filename, we use the *@Value* annotation. Here you can define an expression in the Spring Expression Language (SpEL) how to resolve the value. In the case above, we look up the value in a property source by the key *sbb.spamwords.filename*. This property source is populated by provided property files and the system environment. For this example, you can provide it at runtime with a JVM parameter like:

```
-Dsbb.spamwords.filename= PATH TO words.spam
```

We also need to reflect the changes in the *ControlFlow* class, so create the constructor accordingly to our usage in *SpamAppConfig.controlFlow*. Also, we can remove the *SpamDetectorFactory* inside and use the *spamDetector* received by the constructor. At the end *ControlFlow* should look like:

```
public class ControlFlow {

    private SpamDetector spamDetector = null;

    public ControlFlow(SpamDetector spamDetector) {
        super();
        this.spamDetector = spamDetector;
    }
    public void run(String[] args) throws IOException {
        System.out.println(spamDetector.containsSpam(args[0]));
    }
}
```

Now, we have populated the context and can use our *ControlFlow* in the main application by:

```
context.getBean(ControlFlow.class).run(args);
```

getBean will look up a bean in the context of type *ControlFlow* and return it. It expects to find exactly one match, as in our case now and throws exceptions if not.

On the returned *ControlFlow*, we just call our run method as before.

As you see, with just a few annotations we replaced the factory with a solution we can reuse. Plus, it is more flexible in adding common features like transaction handling. As everything is connected by Spring, it can plug in particular features during runtime. It is possible because Spring creates a proxy for our class. This proxy enables Spring to add features without the need that we must change our classes. It is transparent for us.

However, the proxy has its limits. When a class calls a method on itself, it is not going through the proxy. It only goes through the proxy, when one service calls another service. Of course, both must be maintained by Spring.

Most of the time you will not notice this limit, but if you ever do, you can overcome it by using AspectJ during compile time. Just be aware, this way has its own pros and cons.

The usual way to enable a feature is to set up the module like Spring Data, and then you can use it through various annotations. And with Spring Boot it will become even easier to enable a new feature.

In the next section we are making the configuration even smaller and introducing common annotation you will encounter all the time. But before we continue, let's recap the used annotations so far:

- @Configuration marks a class as a config class

- @Bean marks a method so that its return value is added as a bean to the context

- @Autowired references a bean by type and it is expected to have exact one in the context. It can be omitted like in the version above.

- @Value is a way to inject values hard coded or by using the Spring Expression Language (SpEL), the version we used above will look up the value in the environment

More Magic to Make it Simpler

In this section, we introduce a feature called component scan. It will scan the classpath for classes annotated with a particular set of annotations and add those beans to the context. You enable the feature, by adding the *@ComponentScan* annotation on your *@Configuration* class, in our case *SpamAppConfig*.

```
@Configuration
@ComponentScan
public class SpamAppConfig {

}
```

As you see, we already removed the explicit bean declarations here because we are providing them now with the component scan.

The component scan will search for classes annotated with *@Component* or one of its children. It is set on a *@Configuration* and by default will use the package of the config class as a starting point for the scan. All classes in this package, or any sub-packages are scanned.

- @Component is a generic type for a class to be available as a Spring bean

- @Service indicates a service class, but besides semantics and possible filters there's no difference to a @Component

- @Controller marks a controller for Spring MVC and handles web requests

Let's provide *SimpleSpamDetector* to the context again by adding *@Service*. In the same trip, we move the file loading to its constructor and inject the filename like before, here in the constructor:

```
@Service
public class SimpleSpamDetector implements SpamDetector {

    private List<String> spamWords = new ArrayList<String>();

    public SimpleSpamDetector (

      @Value("${sbb.spamwords.filename}")
      String filename

    ) throws IOException {
        spamWords = Files.readAllLines( Paths.get(filename) );
    }

    //rest omitted
}
```

We do the same on the *ControlFlow*, but use *@Component* instead, and can rerun the application:

```
@Component
public class ControlFlow {
    //rest omitted
}
```

As an exercise, you can do the same with the *RemoteSpamDetector* and finally include it in the context. On the first run, Spring will now complain that you have more than one class of type *SpamDetector* in the context and won't start.

In these situations, you need to specify which of the beans you want. Add the *@Qualifier* annotation to the *spamDetector* parameter in the *ControlFlow* constructor. *@Qualifier* accepts a name of the bean. Spring will now check for a bean with this name and type. When you use the *@Component* annotation, Spring uses the name of the class with the first letter in lowercase as the bean name. Of course, you can also declare your own in an annotation parameter (same as with *@Bean* before):

```
public ControlFlow (

  @Qualifier("simpleSpamDetector")
  SpamDetector spamDetector

) {
    super();
    this.spamDetector = spamDetector;
}
```

In this variant, we can not choose the spam detector implementation during runtime. However, it is possible, but strays away too far from the focus of the book. Nonetheless, I don't want you to leave empty handed, so one solution could be to use the *Application-Context* in your bean. It can be injected like any other bean.

At this point, you have learned the essentials of Spring. Everything Spring does is based on this foundation. When you understood these, the Spring Universe does not look that overwhelming anymore, and you can tackle the rest successfully.

Take your time and play a bit with it to deepen your understanding.

In the next chapter we will start with Spring Boot, what it is and then we are going to develop your first microservice with it.

Recap

Before we continue, let's check your understanding with a short quiz.

- Which problems did our starting application have?

- What's Inversion of Control?

- What is the ApplicationContext?

- How do you set one up?

- How do you register your service or component to the context?

- How can you use a different service?

What Is Spring Boot?

In short, Spring Boot is a new Framework with an opinionated view of building production-ready applications using the standard Spring Framework. Building applications with the Spring Framework used to be a tedious task; especially when starting a new project. Spring consists of multiple modules which you can use individually or integrate each other. The downside is that you always had to do it manually. Also, in many cases, modules were not shipped with default configurations of out the box - they assume you connect them however you like. So, you had to connect everything by yourself too, be it in XML, or with Java annotations. That changed with Spring Boot.

Spring Boot is a way to start new applications and use the world of Spring modules with defaults which make sense.

Its Features:

- Create stand-alone Spring applications; no need for a Servlet Containers or application server - no WAR files.

- Develop Web apps using embedded Tomcat, Jetty or Undertow

- Provide sense-making 'starter' poms to simplify your Maven configuration

- Automatically configure Spring as much as possible

- Production-ready add-ons such as metrics, health checks, and externalized configuration

- No code generation and no requirement for XML configuration - but you can use them, which is important when working with legacy code which itself uses the classic Spring Framework.

- You can even build command line applications with it

Getting Started

The easiest way to start a new project is by using the Spring Initializer (https://start.spring.io/).

The second way is to create a Maven pom.xml file. The pom.xml (referenced from now on as pom) is the instruction file that will be used to build your project. If you are new to Maven, check out the brief introduction to Maven in Appendix A.

Open your text editor and add the following:

```xml
<?xml version="1.0" encoding="UTF-8"?>
<project
  xmlns="http://maven.apache.org/POM/4.0.0"
  xmlns:xsi="http://www.w3.org/2001/XMLSchema-instance"
  xsi:schemaLocation="http://maven.apache.org/POM/4.0.0
  http://maven.apache.org/xsd/maven-4.0.0.xsd">

  <modelVersion>4.0.0</modelVersion>

  <groupId>cde.codeboje.springbootbook</groupId>
  <artifactId>comment-store</artifactId>
  <version>1.0.0-SNAPSHOT</version>

  <parent>
    <groupId>org.springframework.boot</groupId>
    <artifactId>spring-boot-starter-parent</artifactId>
    <version>2.1.8.RELEASE</version>
  </parent>

</project>
```

Spring Boot provides various "Starters" for integrating and auto-configuring other modules of the Spring framework, like the embedded Tomcat. We just need to add the starters as a dependency in the pom file, and Spring Boot will automatically configure it using default values.

Under the hoods, Spring Boot basically does a component scan for *@Configuration* classes like we did in the previous chapter. However, this one is a bit more complex as it also evaluates certain rules for each *@Configuration* found. If the rules pass, the *@Configuration* is loaded, and thus any beans it defines are added to the context. These rules are declared by each starter module and follow a particular scheme.

That's the magic. Furthermore, it is all you need to know if you just want to use it. If you want to learn how to implement your own starter, check out the books resource page.

For a web application, we will need the *spring-boot-starter-web* which will embed a Tomcat and Spring MVC and configures everything so you can just write your Spring MVC Controllers.

Let's add it to the pom:

```
<dependencies>
  <dependency>
    <groupId>org.springframework.boot</groupId>
    <artifactId>spring-boot-starter-web</artifactId>
  </dependency>
</dependencies>
```

The next step is to tell Spring Boot how to initialize our application. A Spring Boot application is in its essence a simple Java program with a main method. In it, we need to use the SpringApplication entry point and start it by calling the *run* method. This will bootstrap our application and sprinkle everything with Spring Boot fairy dust aka auto-configure a Tomcat web server, Spring MVC, and serves our application.

We annotate our main class with the *@SpringBootApplication* annotation to configure Spring Boot. It is a shortcut for the annotations *@Configuration*, *@ComponentScan*, and *@EnableAutoConfiguration*.

- @Configuration marks a class as a Java based configuration

- @ComponentScan scans the classpath for particular Spring annotated classes

- @EnableAutoConfiguration enables the auto-configuration of Spring Boot

The first two are the same as we covered in the previous chapter and the last one enables the auto-configuration. So, instead of adding those three individually to the application, we can use *@SpringBootApplication* as the shortcut.

```
package de.codeboje.springbootbook.commentstore;
import org.springframework.boot.*;
import org.springframework.boot.autoconfigure.*;
import org.springframework.stereotype.*;

@SpringBootApplication
public class CommentStoreApp {

    public static void main(String[] args) throws Exception {
        SpringApplication.run( CommentStoreApp.class, args );
    }

}
```

The main class, *CommentStoreApp*, is, therefore, a *@Configuration* itself and you can add custom beans in the same way as we did before. Or, you can take advantage of the component scan as we will do.

Now you can run it either as a Java application (STS: Run as Java Application) or by using Maven with *mvn spring-boot:run*. Of course, it doesn't do anything right now; so let's add a simple web endpoint.

Set the *@RestController* on the *CommentStoreApp* class from above and add the method:

```
@RequestMapping("/")
String home() {
    return "Hello World!";
}
```

The Annotation will mark our class as a Spring MVC Controller providing a restful endpoint. Spring Boot recognizes it and will set up Spring MVC and a default JSON transformation using the Jackson library.

The *RequestMapping* annotation on the new method provides routing information for Spring MVC. The root path of our application is tied to this method, i.e.- when you later access the application in the browser, Spring will know it must call our *home* method for fulfilling the request. We will cover this more in the Rest API chapter.

Rerun the example and open your web browser to localhost:8080 and you should see a "Hello World!".

To exit the application, hit ctrl-c.

Voila! Your first Spring Boot app.

But that's only a toy application. Starting with the next chapter, we will build our sample application.

Recap

Before we continue, let's check your understanding with a short quiz.

- Is the main application also a @Configuration class?

- For which annotations is @SpringBootApplication a shortcut?

- How does the auto-configuration work?

Data Access Layer With Spring Data JPA

In this chapter, we are going to implement our persistence layer.

For that, we are going to use the Spring Data JPA Framework. Spring Data is an umbrella project to make working with data stores easier and encapsulate the actual data storage access— meaning you could switch the database backend without changing a single line of your data access code. However, the primary purpose is to provide Spring users a stable interface for working with data storages regardless of the real storage used, but still allow the use of specific traits of the storage. In case of Spring Data JPA, the backend is JPA, the Java Persistence API, and behind that any supported relational database. As JPA itself is only a specification, Spring Data JPA uses Hibernate as the implementation. However, your application code interacts with Spring Data JPA and doesn't work with the JPA techniques directly.

To use it in our application we need to add the dependency to the spring boot starter:

```
<dependency>
  <groupId>org.springframework.boot</groupId>
  <artifactId>spring-boot-starter-data-jpa</artifactId>
</dependency>
```

Next we need to tell Spring Boot which database we are going to use. The first thing we add is the database JDBC driver as a dependency to the pom. For the sake of simplicity we are going to use the embedded in-memory database H2, but in a real world scenario, it can be any SQL JDBC Driver.

```
<dependency>
  <groupId>com.h2database</groupId>
  <artifactId>h2</artifactId>
</dependency>
```

When we use H2, HSQL, or Derby as an embedded database, Spring Boot takes care of setting up the whole access layer, so whenever we use a different database we must define access to the database. We set those configurations in a properties file named *application.properties*.

When we introduced the *@Value* annotation earlier, I mentioned that its values are filled by a property source. This is populated by environment variables and Java properties files. Usually, when using Spring alone, we had to manually define a property source in the context and specify any property file to use.
Spring Boot does this automatically and will include values from a *application.properties* or *application.yml* file. The latter uses YAML instead; both are equally handled. By default, it will look for those two in the classpath.

Create the file under *src/main/resources* and add the following section:

```
spring.datasource.url=jdbc:h2:mem:mydb
spring.datasource.username=sa
```

spring.datasource.url tells Spring Boot where the database is located and which driver to use. It follows standard JDBC URL naming scheme.

spring.datasource.username is the username to access the database. In the case of an in-memory DB, we do not need a password, but it would be defined with the property *spring.datasource.password*.

In case we would use PostgreSQL as the backend, the previous section could look like:

```
spring.datasource.url=jdbc:postgresql://localhost:5432/commentstore
spring.datasource.username=postgres
spring.datasource.password=password
```

When we start our application now, database access is automatically configured and ready to go. The only thing missing is the database itself, but we can let Hibernate create it by adding the following to our *application.properties*:

```
spring.jpa.hibernate.ddl-auto=update
```

The property *spring.jpa.hibernate.ddl-auto* defines if and when Hibernate will create our database with all tables; in our case we let it update the schema every time we start the application.

HINT: Don't do that in production. Track database changes manually. This auto mechanism can backfire if you have forgotten something or an unforeseen issue arises. In the worst case scenario, your data is permanently erased. In my last project, we had a case in which someone did that and accidentally killed the whole production database - no fun at all.

The auto-configuration of the Spring Data JPA starter scans for known database drivers in the classpath and if found, will set up a JDBC *Datasource* and the *EntityManager* and *EntityManagerFactory* of JPA and add them to the context. It also scans for *@Entity* classes and builds the configuration needed for the *EntityManager*.

Specific features of Hibernate or JPA can be configured using the regular *application.properties* file. They are grouped under the prefix *spring.jpa* and *spring.jpa.hibernate*.

Creating Our Entity

Usually, JPA Entity classes are specified in a *persistence.xml* file, but with Spring Boot we do not need that tedious task anymore and can use the entity scan. By default all packages below the configuration class, in our case, *CommentStoreApp*, will be scanned for classes annotated with *@Entity*, *@Embeddable* or *@MappedSuperclass*. If they reside in a different package, we must add *@EntityScan* explicitly to our configuration class.

As we have placed the model class in a different package (on purpose), we need to insert the following line to our *CommentStoreApp* configuration:

```
@EntityScan(basePackages= {
  "de.codeboje.springbootbook"
})
```

Spring Boot now scans all packages starting from *de.codeboje.springbootbook* for our entity classes. So create the class *Comment* in the package *de.codeboje.springbootbook.model* . Imports and get/setter are omitted for readability.

```
@Entity
@Table(
  name = "comments_model",
  indexes = {
            @Index(name = "idx_pageId",
                    columnList = "pageId"
            )
  }
)
public class Comment implements Serializable {

    @Id
    @Column(length = 36)
    private String id;

    @Version
    private Integer version;

    @Column(columnDefinition = "TEXT")
    private String comment;

    @Column(length = 32)
    private String pageId;

    @Column(length = 32)
    private String username;

    @Column(length = 32)
    private String emailAddress;

    @Column
    private boolean spam;

    private Instant lastModificationDate;

    private Instant creationDate;
```

Let's look at the annotations involved:

- @Entity: Tells Hibernate and Spring that this is our Entity class.

- @Table: defines a table name and sets an index on the pageId; we will query later on it.

- @Id: Unique ID of our Comment record, we will manually assign the id, for auto generated values you would use a Long as the field type and add the @Generated-Value annotation.

- @Version: A version ID used by Hibernate for optimistic locking.

- @Column: Used for changing column names or setting field length, etc. is optional.

What happens now in the background is that JPA in the form of Hibernate creates an SQL schema for our class and populates it with all our fields respecting the annotations we used above. It also uses these definitions for mapping between SQL and object and vice versa.

The model is a simple POJO (plain old Java object), and the fields are pretty self-explanatory, so we leave them as is.

When we start our application, Spring Boot will detect our *@Entity* class, set up our database access using JPA and Hibernate, and Hibernate will create our database and table. In the end, we are ready to use our model.

Storing and Retrieving Data Using the Spring Data JPA Repositories

Now that we have built our model let's use it.

The central part of data access in Spring Data is the *Repository* interface. In it, we define an interface declaring our queries and Spring Data will do the rest like the actual data retrieval and storage.

When our application starts, Spring Data will create a proxy for our interface. This proxy handles all the logic to work with our data and behaves like a regular Spring bean, i.e.- it is available in the context, and we can inject it. For our application code, it is just another interface we code against. But it is best understood by using it.

In our repository interface, we can define our queries either by a naming convention for the method name or explicit with the Spring Data JPA Query annotation *@Query*. When using the *@Query* annotation, we write our query in the JPQL (Java Persistence Query Language); it looks similar to SQL, but works on objects.

Besides the basic *Repository*, there are some sub-classes with more predefined methods, e.g.- the *CrudRepository* offering support for basic Create-Retrieve-Update-Delete operations.

By default, all packages below the configuration class, in our case *CommentStoreApp*, are scanned for *Repository* interfaces. If the repositories reside in another package, we must use *@EnableJpaRepositories* on the *@Configuration* class and define the base package in the same way as with *@EntityScan*.

Create our *CommentRepository* in *de.codeboje.springbootbook.commentstore.service* and extend the *CrudRepository* interface.:

```
public interface CommentRepository extends CrudRepository<Comment, String> {

//    @Query("select a from Comment a where a.pageId = ?1")
    List<Comment> findByPageId(String pageId);

    List<Comment> findByPageIdAndSpamIsTrue(String pageId);
}
```

First, *Repository* and its children require two generic types. The first declares the model class and the second one the primary key. In our case, it is *Comment* for the model, and the primary key is a *String*.

Second, we use the naming scheme approach and tell Spring Data we search for all records with a particular pageId. And as a result, we will retrieve a *List* of *Comment*. More on return types in a minute.

A method using the naming convention starts with a prefix followed by a *By* as a delimiter and then the actual properties with additional support of AND, OR, etc. The real value of a property is passed as a method parameter in the same order.

- Prefixes: find, count, read, query or get

- Delimiter: By

- Query: property names and AND, OR, etc.; for a full list see query creation section of the Spring Data JPA documentation

Examples:

```
findByPageId(String pageId)

queryByPageId(String pageId)

findByPageIdAndSpamIsTrue(String pageId)
```

The advantages of the naming scheme are it's straight forward to define basic queries and it has a common set of query keywords supported by all Spring Data backends, i.e.- the method name is the same regardless if we use JPA, or MongoDB, etc. However, it also has disadvantages of becoming hardly readable for longer queries, and we have to refactor our code if you ever change a method name. The latter might not be a problem depending on your particular component infrastructure.

We could also have used the *@Query* annotation and write our query in the JPQL (Java Persistence Query Language) like:

```
@Query("select a from Comment a where a.pageId = ?1")
```

The JPQL is like SQL for objects and as powerful. We are not covering the JPQL here, but rather how to use it with Spring Data.

In our query, we can reference parameters either by their positions in the method signature of by assigning a name.

When referencing a parameter by position, we use a *?* follow by the position of the parameter in the query. Positions start at 1.

To reference a parameter by name we can use *:* followed by the parameter name in the JPQL. However, we must define a mapping for Spring Data and thus add the *@Param* to the parameter in the method signature like:

```
@Query("select a from Comment a where a.pageId = :pageId")
List<Comment> findByPageId(@Param("pageId") String thePageId);
```

When Spring Data now calls JPA internally, it will supply our parameter *thePageId* as a JPA parameter named *pageId*.

If we hit the limits when querying by naming scheme, we also have the option to use the power of JPQL directly.

Regardless of the query type, we can define a return type. Spring Data supports a few, but we stick to the essentials here.

For queries returning a single type, we can directly return our model or use the Java 8 *Optional* for null-safety. The methods provided by one of the *Repository* children will use *Optional*.

When returning multiple values, we can use *List, Collection, Stream, Page* or, like in the default methods, a *Iterable*.

We now have set up our database access, our model, queries and are now ready to use it. The next thing we must do is to inject our repository into a service class and finally create some comments. Precisely this and also some testing, we will cover in the next chapter.

Special Query Parameters

The Spring Data *Repository* interface supports pagination and sorting out of the box. All we need to do is, add a parameter to our query method and use one of the special types as the parameter. Spring Data will do the rest.

- Pageable is an interface defining a request for a page with number of the page, how many items per page and an optional sorting

- Sort defines sorting for the query; is also used in the Pageable

Only one of them is allowed per method because the *Pageable* already includes sorting and it wouldn't make sense to add it separately.

In our *CommentRepository* it could look like:

```
Page<Comment> findByPageId(String pageId, Pageable pageable);

List<Comment> findByPageId(String pageId, Sort sort);
```

When we use a *Pageable*, we usually do not want a full result list, which could be huge, but rather the results for a particular page. For that, we change the return type from *List* to *Page*.

Page contains the actual result of records and some additional meta data like total matches, number of pages, items per page, etc. Its content ,aka our records, is accessible with *getContent*.

By using *Pageable* and *Page* together, we get pagination out of the box. No need to stitch it together manually.

Tips

When developing on a larger scale, some settings are pretty helpful.

See the SQL Sent to Our DB

With more complex models, I often had the need to see the SQL query Spring actually builds and sends to the database. We can see it by adding:

```
spring.jpa.show-sql=true
```

to our *application.properties*. The statements are logged out on stdout and/or our configured logging.

Preventing Errors on Dead DB Connections

The underlying logic usually accesses our database with some kind of connection pool. If our code needs to send a query, it gets a connection from the pool, and when it is done, it gives it back. However, what can happen due to network issues, DB timeouts, etc., is that the connection gets stale. If the connection is stale, it is essentially dead and can not be used. Typically, the pool does not clean them up, and the next time we use a connection, it might hand us the broken one. However, we can tell the pool to check each connection before using it.

To enable that add the following section to our *application.properties*:

```
spring.datasource.test-on-borrow=true
spring.datasource.validation-query=SELECT 1
```

spring.datasource.test-on-borrow enables the check for valid connections
spring.datasource.validation-query defines a query for the check.

The check does come with a drawback, though– a minor loss in performance. Depending on a particular scenario, it might be noticeable.

Recap

Before we continue, let's review what we have covered and check your understanding with a short quiz.

- Which Start do we use for Spring Data JPA?

- What steps are needed for using an H2 DB?

- Where do you configure the database URL and credentials?

- Where does Spring Boot look by default for JPA Entity classes?

- How can you specify a model in a different package?

- How can you see the SQL going to your database?

Implementing the Service Layer

In this chapter, we are going to implement our service layer. It will store and retrieve our data using the repository we created in the previous chapter and we will use the *Spam-Detector* service from the beginning.

In the main route we will include the *SpamDetector* service with a component scan and at the end of the chapter I will show you briefly a second way by using XML; in case you ever have to work with legacy Spring configs. The variant using XML is the way I used in the source code on GitHub.

Our Service Interface

Create the *CommentService* interface in the *de.codeboje.springbootbook.commentstore.service* package and define the following methods:

```
public interface CommentService {

    String put(Comment model) throws IOException;

    List<Comment> list(String pageId) throws IOException;

    Comment get(String id);

    List<Comment> listSpamComments(String pageId) throws IOException;

    void delete(String id);

}
```

It defines a method for storing a comment *put*, to delete a comment *delete*, retrieve a single comment *get*, and getting a list of comments *list* a specific page.

Our Service Class

Our Service will use the *SpamDetector* service we developed before. First, we must install it in our local Maven repository by running a *mvn clean install*. If we don't do it, Maven can't resolve the dependency for us and thus we can not use it in our new *CommentService*.

Next, we add it as a dependency finally to the pom:

```
<dependency>
  <groupId>de.codeboje.springbootbook</groupId>
  <artifactId>spam-detection</artifactId>
  <version>1.0.0-SNAPSHOT</version>
</dependency>
```

The next step is to create our service class implementing our previously defined interface:

```
@Service
public class CommentServiceImpl implements CommentService {

    @Autowired
    private SpamDetector spamDetector;

    @Autowired
    private CommentRepository repository;

}
```

First, we tell Spring with the *@Service* annotation that this is a service class and it should be initialized and made available for the other components.

Next, we create a variable for our *CommentRepository* as we are going to access data. The *@Autowired* annotation tells Spring to auto wire this field, so it will look for ONE instance in its context which implements the *CommentRepository*. The actual implementation of the interface is created during startup by Spring Data.

We do the same with our spam detector module. It provides exactly one interface, *Spam-Detector*. If we started the application now, Spring would complain that it does not find a class implementing the *SpamDetector* interface.

Setting up the SpamDetector Service

Our *SpamDetector* will check for spam words in a text. The words are defined in a plain text file with each unwanted word on its own line. Go ahead; create the file in *src/main/resources/* of the commentstore and fill it with a few words or use the version we created earlier.

The *SimpleSpamDetector* is annotated with *@Service* and would be picked up with the component scan of the *CommentStoreApp* if it is in a sub-package. Chances are, it is not, so let's adjust the component scan.

Open our *CommentStoreApp* and add:

```
@ComponentScan(
  basePackages= {
    "de.codeboje.springbootbook",
    "de.codeboje.springbootbook.spamdetection"
  }
)
```

to the class. This will instruct the *@ComponentScan* to search the two declared packages. First, is the main package of our application and the second is the package of the *Spam-Detector*. If we define the *basePackages*, it will only scan those - the default behavior to use the packages of the *@Configuration* is turned off.

In the previous spam checker application, we provided the file name on the command line. Now, we are adding it as a property to our *application.properties*.

```
sbb.spamwords.filename=src/main/resources/words.spam
```

Run the commentstore and it should start without errors.

Adding a Comment

Our *CommentService* interface provides one method for adding or updating a new entry. The caller will send a full *Comment*, and we need to decide if we create a new entry, or update an existing one. The entry is identified by the ID property.

First, we need to check and retrieve an existing entry. As we will work with the retrieved entry anyway and it is pretty small, we directly load it.

To load an entry by Id, we use the *findById* (pre 2 Version: *findOne*) method provided by our repository; it is one of the methods provided by the *CrudRepositry* and takes exactly one argument - the ID of the record:

```
repository.findById(id)
```

Implement it as the get method and add:

```
@Override
public Comment get(String id) {
    return repository.findById(id).orElse(null);
}
```

to our service implementation. *findById* returns a Java 8 *Optional* with our model inside. However, in the example, we just return the value in the *Optional* or null if we didn't find our comment.

The *CrudRepositry* defines one method for saving; if the comment with this ID already exists, it will be overridden otherwise it will create a new comment.

Creating a new one is as simple as:

```
repository.save(model);
```

Spring Data JPA takes the model class and serializes it to the database; overriding any existing record with the new data. Except when the version property differs. Then it will throw an exception that the database record was modified, e.g.- in another request - it is called optimistic locking. It is the default behavior here and works most of the time. However, we can adjust it in Hibernate but that is a topic of its own.

Our method for adding or updating looks like:

```
@Override
@Transactional
public String put(Comment model) throws IOException {

    if (StringUtils.isEmpty(model.getId())) {
        model.setId(UUID.randomUUID().toString());
    }
    if(spamDetector.containsSpam(model.getUsername())
        || spamDetector.containsSpam(model.getEmailAddress())
        || spamDetector.containsSpam(model.getComment())
    ) {
        model.setSpam(true);
    }

    final Comment dbModel = get(model.getId());
    if (dbModel != null) {
        dbModel.setUsername(model.getUsername());
        dbModel.setComment(model.getComment());
        dbModel.setLastModificationDate(
          Instant.now()
        );
        repository.save(dbModel);
    }
    else {
        model.setCreationDate(Instant.now());
        model.setLastModificationDate(
          Instant.now()
        );
        repository.save(model);
    }
    return model.getId();
}
```

If the comment already has an ID, our service will update it. If it does not have one, we will create the ID by ourselves. Next, we check the *username, emailAddress,* and *comment* fields for spam and if the service detects any, the comment is marked as spam.

In either case, for storing our database model, we use the *repository.save* method.

Transaction Management

When working with complex models or different backends we usually need some transaction handling. So if anything goes wrong in one backend, we can roll back our data in all.

The Spring Family also provides a module for transaction management *Spring Transaction Management*. It is used in Spring Data, and we can enable the basic version in two simple steps.

First, annotate our method with *@Transactional* like in our version above and second, enable it in the Spring Boot Configuration by adding the *@EnableTransactionManagement* annotation to *CommentStoreApp*.

That's the power of a Spring proxy in action. We don't change our class for transaction handling, we just tell Spring Data that it should wrap our method with a transaction. And it does.

If our method fails with an exception, Spring Data will initiate a rollback on the transaction manager. By default, Spring Data JPA is setup automatically in Spring Boot to support this when we enable transaction handling with the *@EnableTransactionManagement* annotation.

Writing Tests for the Service

Spring Boot provides an easy starter dependency which includes Spring Boot Test modules and a handful of useful libraries like JUnit, Hamcrest, and co.

Add the following section to our pom, and we can start to write a test:

```
<dependency>
    <groupId>org.springframework.boot</groupId>
    <artifactId>spring-boot-starter-test</artifactId>
    <scope>test</scope>
</dependency>
```

The Spring Test modules use JUnit at its core but enhance it to make use of the dependency injections of Spring.

Create *CommentstoreServiceImplTest* in *src/test/java* and let's start with implementing a test.

First, we need to tell JUnit that we use the Spring Feature:

```
@RunWith(SpringRunner.class)
```

Second, we must set up our Spring Boot application for testing. The easiest way is to annotate the class with:

```
@SpringBootTest()
```

The Spring Boot test feature now auto configures our application completely as it would run later but also induces some testing functions. So, any Spring Bean, either set up by our configuration or found with a *ComponentScan*, will be available in the Spring Context. If the application uses a lot, it might slow down the test runs.

But, if our data access object or service does not have any dependencies except JPA, we can use the *@DataJpaTest* annotation instead. Spring Boot will now only scan for *@Entity* classes and configure Spring Data JPA repositories. All other *@Component* beans are ignored for the *ApplicationContext* of this test.

Be aware though, that certain features like the *@Value* injection are only set up by using the *@SpringBootTest*, or we have to do it manually.

Now that our test is initialized through Spring, we can use dependency injection in our test, i.e.- we can auto wire our *CommentRepository*.

For our test, we will set up an in-memory database and use this for storing the comments. As tests should run independently, we clear our table before each test run. When using *@DataJpaTest*, we can skip this step as in this case, our test method is wrapped in a transaction which is automatically rolled back at the end.

We are lazy and use the same model values for the whole test:

```
@Before
public void setup() {
    model = new Comment();
    model.setUsername("testuser");
    model.setId("dqe345e456rf34rw");
    model.setPageId("product0815");
    model.setEmailAddress("example@example.com");
    model.setComment("I am the comment");
    repository.deleteAll();
}
```

Now we can create a JUnit test by annotating the method with *@Test* and implement it using our injected service:

```
@Test
public void testListNotFound() throws IOException {
    service.put(model);
    List<Comment> r = service.list("notfound");
    assertTrue(r.isEmpty());
}
```

The rest of the process is basic JUnit testing, and we can use all features that the framework has to offer.

Alternative: Adding a Legacy Module With Its Own Spring XML Configuration

When we work with modules which have pre-configured Spring configurations in XML, we can simply import them with the *@ImportResource* annotation. It is used on the *@Configuration* of our application. The example in the GitHub repository is using the XML import approach.

The legacy module uses its own Spring XML configuration where it is setup and ready to use as a black box. It includes a bean definition for our *SpamDetector* and also makes use of a spring property, so we need to set this one up, too. Remember this is a stripped down version for demonstration purposes, in real world cases they are more complex.

```xml
<?xml version="1.0" encoding="UTF-8"?>
<beans
  xmlns= "http://www.springframework.org/schema/beans"
  xmlns:xsi= "http://www.w3.org/2001/XMLSchema-instance"
  xsi:schemaLocation= "http://www.springframework.org/schema/beans http://
www.springframework.org/schema/beans/spring-beans.xsd">

  <bean id="legacySpamDetector"
    class= "de.codeboje.springbootbook.spamdetection.impl.SimpleSpamDetector"
  >
    <constructor-arg>
      <value>${sbb.spamwords.filename}</value>
    </constructor-arg>
  </bean>
</beans>
```

The configuration is packed in the jar file of the legacy module so that we can use it directly.

Open our *CommentStoreApp* and add:

```
@ImportResource(value={"classpath*:legacy-context.xml"})
```

to the class. The *@ImportResource* will validate the mentioned context and include it in the current one thus making all the beans in it available. By default, it will look in the current project, but with prepending *classpath** Spring searches the whole classpath for our file at the root position.

Next, we must define the *sbb.spamwords.filename* property in our *application.properties* like before. Rerun the application and it should start without problems.

Recap

Before we continue, let's review what we have covered and check your understanding with a short quiz.

- How can you include an existing Spring Configuration XML File?

- How do you make your service class available to Spring?

- Where are Spring Properties configured?

- What steps must you take to include Transaction management?

- Can you use Spring dependency injection in JUnit tests? How do you set it up?

In the next chapter, we are going to expose our service in a Rest API.

Implementing the REST API

In this chapter, we are going to implement a REST API for our service using Spring MVC. It is more REST-like because we are not following the Hypermedia approach entirely. However, we'll name it REST API regardless of what the hypermedia police thinks.

Spring MVC is Spring Frameworks' answer for developing web applications. It is based around a central *DispatcherServlet* and controllers implementing the actual request handling. When a request enters the system, it is first handled by the *DispatcherServlet*, The *DispatcherServlet* will now determine which controller method is responsible for handling this request and when it finds the right one, it forwards the request accordingly. Now, the controller takes over, does whatever logic it contains, and returns a result which is then send back as a response. The response can either be plain JSON, XML, or we use any of the server side template engines and return an HTML page.

What a controller actually does, is up to us as it is the central point we must provide for when building a web application with Spring MVC.

We will separate our API in two use cases and classes:

- Retrieving comments

- Writing and deleting comments

A typical REST API makes an instance of your model available under its own URL. Interaction, like retrieving or deleting, is all done using the same endpoint, but with different HTTP request methods:

- GET for retrieving

- POST for creating

- PUT for changing

- DELETE for deleting

However, there are no fixed rules and you can use whatever makes more sense in your applications. Creating an instance is regularly handled under one single endpoint as the ID will mostly be created on the service side.

In our sample application, we will use the single endpoint approach for creating comments and deleting them under their own endpoint. Retrieving a single comment does not make sense here. Thus we are providing an endpoint for retrieving all comments of a particular page.

To use Spring MVC in our Spring Boot application, we must add the Starter to our pom file:

```
<dependency>
  <groupId>org.springframework.boot</groupId>
  <artifactId>spring-boot-starter-web</artifactId>
</dependency>
```

As we have enabled auto-configuration before (@*SpringBootApplication*) Spring Boot will detect the web starter and set it up accordingly. Essentially, it configures Spring MVC, scans for controller classes, and runs everything inside an embedded Tomcat by default.

Before we dive into the REST API, we'll introduce a simple helper feature during development. Spring Boot offers a dev tools module, which basically enables hot code reloading and depending on some starter other behavior.

For enabling this feature, we must add only its dependency to our pom:

```
<dependency>
  <groupId>org.springframework.boot</groupId>
  <artifactId>spring-boot-devtools</artifactId>
  <optional>true</optional>
</dependency>
```

When we start the application now and change some code while running, it will reload our application. However, this feature has its limits so in case you experience strange problems, restart the application manually.

Another feature is an integrated database viewer for the H2 database. It can be accessed in the browser at *h2-console* and logged in using the credentials from the data access chapter.

REST API Implementation

In Spring MVC the main component we need to implement is a controller class. The dispatching mechanism in Spring MVC will eventually call a method on your controller class to fulfill the request. It determines the right controller method by:

- the request path

- the content type an endpoint returns

- the content type the sender (e.g., browser) sends with the Accept header

- the content type an endpoint accepts for input (like JSON, forms, etc.)

When Spring MVC can not detect a suitable endpoint, it will write an error in the logs and response with an HTPP status code 415 - Unsupported Media Type.

Controller classes are plain Java objects which are annotated with the *@Controller* Annotation. Spring MVC scans during startup for classes with the *@Controller* annotation and will register them.

Next, we need to inform Spring MVC which method in our controller maps to which endpoint in our application. We can do this with the *@RequestMapping* annotation on a method.

So much for the basic theory; let's dive into the actual implementation now.

Write Operations

Create the new class *WriteController* in the *de.codeboje.springbootbook.commentstore.restapi* package and then add the *@Controller* annotation on the class level. Moreover, while we are at it, we will directly add our *CommentService* service and let Spring auto wire it:

```
@Controller
public class WriteController {

    @Autowired
    private CommentService service;
}
```

In the next step, we declare our first endpoint. We post a new comment in our sample application with an HTTP Form Post.

With the *@RequestMapping*, Spring knows that this is an endpoint. The *value* parameter is the path under which this method is made available, and the *method* parameter defines that we only accept HTTP Post request. Both parameters are set on the annotation.

MVC provides multiple ways to map from incoming parameters to our method parameters and their types.

To map a simple form field or URL parameter, we can annotate our method parameter with *@RequestParam* and set the matching name on the annotation. This will look like:

```
public @ResponseBody String create(
    @RequestParam("comment") final String comment
) {
    //rest omitted
}
```

We could do this for all of our comment fields, but in this case there is a short way. Instead of the *@RequestParam*, we use the *@ModelAttribute* annotation and directly use our *Comment* model as the parameter type. MVC will not map each form field to a model field by name, i.e.- Input name is *comment* and in *Comment* must be a field named *comment* or better a setter for it; it follows the Java Beans way.

When we implement it, it looks like:

```
@RequestMapping( value = "/comments", method = RequestMethod.POST )
@ResponseStatus( value = HttpStatus.CREATED )
public @ResponseBody String create( @ModelAttribute Comment model )
  throws IOException
{
```

```
      return service.put(model);
}
```

Usually when we return a String value in our method, Spring MVC will look up a view (aka template) to forward the request to. Depending on your configuration you can use plain old JSPs or any of the newer template engines for that. You can find more about it in the Spring documentation (see resource page).

In our case, we just want to return the ID of the created comment as plain text, so we will use the *@ResponseBody* annotation on the return value. MVC will now return our object as a plain string. The format the object is returned is determined by a *ContentNegotationStrategy*, and the actual conversion is done by an HTTP message converter, e.g.- to JSON, to XML. It is the same mechanism as we used before for mapping request input to our model.

The *@RequestMapping* has a *produces* parameter that defines which format the endpoint will return. Using the values of the *@RequestMapping* annotation and by analyzing the request, Spring MVC decides which converter to use. To keep it simple, in our case MVC will fallback to plain String conversion.

@ResponseStatus is an annotation to change the HTTP status code of a response. In REST APIs it is usually a 201 - Created instead of a regular 200 - OK when we created a new instance of our model.

Our method now receives an instance of our *Comment*, calls our service to add it, and returns the ID of the comment. The ID is wrapped with an HTTP response and returned to the client.

As an exercise, you can implement the comment delete and make the endpoint available under */comment/{id}*.

Integration Testing

How can we confirm that it works? By testing it and we will start with a Unit test.

Create the *WriteControllerTest* under *src/test/java* in the package *de.codeboje.springbootbook.commentstore.restapi*. Now we configure it with *@RunWith* and *@SpringBootTest* like in the previous chapter, so Spring Test has the right context.

The test could run now but would start an embedded servlet container, just as in a regular application start. Depending on our application and our test runtime environment it might be better to test only in a mock web environment. To enable it, we only need to add *webEnvironment = WebEnvironment.MOCK* to the *@SpringBootTest* annotation. Now Spring Boot Test runs our test with a mock web environment, and we can test using Spring MVC Test.

The main helper of Spring MVC Test is *MockMvc*, and it provides methods to interact with *@Controller* via the mock web environment. In earlier versions of Spring Boot you had to set this one up manually, but now we just need to add the *@AutoConfigureMockMvc* annotation to the test, and voila! *MockMvc* can be injected like any other regular Spring Bean and is ready to use.

If we are going to test only the *@Controller*, we could also use *@WebMvcTest* instead of *@SpringBootTest* as an alternative. This will only set up our web configuration for an MVC mock environment and ignores all other *@Component* beans. To provide mocks for depending service classes, we can use the *@MockBean* annotation feature in the test class. Simply set it on a field in the test like:

```
@MockBean
private CommentService service;
```

Spring Boot Test provides you a Mockito mock for it. Besides, it also resets the mock after each test method.

We will write an integration test for the *WriteController* and use the *@WebMvcTest* feature later for testing the ReadController (#readcontrollertest).

Let's start.

```
@SpringBootTest(webEnvironment = WebEnvironment.MOCK)
@AutoConfigureMockMvc
public class WriteControllerTest {
```

```
        @Autowired
        private WebApplicationContext context;

        @Autowired
        private CommentService service;

        @Autowired
        private MockMvc mvc;
}
```

Now it is ready to use, and we can create our first test. Create the test method and add the *@Test* annotation from JUnit.

To call a web method on the mock we use the perform method. It needs a *RequestBuilder* which knows how to build a specific request, in our case one for form posts. *MockMvc-RequestBuilders.post* builds it and will point it at the */comments* endpoint. *MockMvc-RequestBuilders* also contains methods for the other request types.

Now on the *RequestBuilder*, we can set our form fields with the *param* method.

When called, *perform* will now execute our request in the Spring Test black box.

The *perform* method also returns a *ResultActions* where we can chain individual tests and validate if the request was successful.

For example:

```
andExpect(status().is(200))
```

Read it as "We expect that the result has a status code of 200".

We will cover the *andExpect* syntax in the test section of our *ReadController* a bit more.

As we want to check that our comment is actually created, we will load it directly via the *CommentRepository*. But for that, we require the ID returned by the REST API. To access it Spring Test provides the *andReturn() ResultActions*, which will return a class for working with the result.

To retrieve the ID as a plain String, we get the actual response from the result and use the *getContentAsString* on this:

```
result.getResponse().getContentAsString()
```

As we only return one single string, we are ready to use it as it is.

Put together, our test looks like:

```
@Test
public void testPost() throws Exception {

    Comment model = setupDummyModel();

    MvcResult result = this.mvc.perform(
      MockMvcRequestBuilders.post("/create")
      .param("comment", model.getComment())
      .param("pageId", model.getPageId())
      .param("emailAddress", model.getEmailAddress())
      .param("username", model.getUsername())
    )
     .andExpect(status().is(200))
     .andReturn();

    String id = result.getResponse().getContentAsString();
    Comment dbModel = service.get(id);
    assertNotNull(dbModel);
    assertEquals(model.getComment(), dbModel.getComment());
    assertEquals(model.getPageId(), dbModel.getPageId());
    assertEquals(model.getUsername(), dbModel.getUsername());
    assertEquals(model.getEmailAddress(), dbModel.getEmailAddress());

    assertNotNull(dbModel.getLastModificationDate());
    assertNotNull(dbModel.getCreationDate());
    assertFalse(model.isSpam());
}
```

To verify that our REST API and service worked, we retrieve the newly created model and compare them to our input. There should be no difference.

In this section, we used an integration test which made more sense than just testing the REST API methods. Of course, we can do pure Unit testing and provide a mock object of our service class using Mockito or similar. That is up to you, your product and context.

Now, as an exercise, you can implement a test for deleting a comment.

Read Operations

Create the new class *ReadController* in the *de.codeboje.springbootbook.commentstore.restapi* package and then add the *@RestController* annotation on the class level. Moreover, while we are at it, we can directly add our *CommentService* service and let Spring auto wire it.

The *@RestController* extends the regular *@Controller* annotation and triggers some additional configurations in Spring MVC. Our endpoint will be set up as a REST endpoint and by default accepting JSON requests and returning JSON as results.

@RestController is a shortcut, and we can archive the same result by using the regular *@Controller* annotation and adding @ResponseBody to your service method and setting the *produces* to *application/json"* on the *@RequestMapping* annotation of your method.

```
@RestController
public class ReadController {

    @Autowired
    private CommentService service;
}
```

By default Spring MVC uses the Jackson library for mapping from JSON to Java object and vice versa.

Retrieving Comments

Receiving comments is straight forward too:

```
@RequestMapping(value = "/comments/{id}")
public List<Comment> getComments(@PathVariable(value = "id") String pageId)
throws IOException {
    List<Comment> r = service.list(pageId);
```

```
        if (r.isEmpty()) {
            throw new FileNotFoundException("/list/" + pageId);
        }
        return r;
    }
```

Our endpoint accepts a variable in its path. Variables in the path are put in curly brackets like *{id}*. We map this one to our method parameter by adding the *@PathVariable* annotation to the method parameter and defining the variable name on it, e.g.- *id*. This mechanism is similar to the *@RequestParam* annotation we used before, but looks up the value in the path of our endpoint and not in the request's parameters. Note: a *@PathVariable* is mandatory. If you send a request to that endpoint without the path variable, it is a different endpoint for Spring.

The method itself simply looks up the comments and returns the result.

As an exercise, you can implement the second request in the *ReadController* and return the spam comments for a page. If in doubt, you can always check my implementation in the source repository.

HINT: We use our business model *Comment* here directly as it is a regular Java Bean. But when you also implement a client lib for in-house or even external use cases, you should be careful with moving the model to a commons lib. If you do it, be aware the client needs all dependencies of your class, and annotations count as such. So each application using our model class will also need all the JPA and Spring annotations we used. This dependency clutter can cause trouble and strange side effects. An alternative would be to use some Domain transfer object (DTO) or not doing a common lib at all. It depends on your context; be aware of it and choose wisely.

Pagination

We already covered pagination on the side of Spring Data. However, its support is not limited to repositories as we can also get smooth support for it in our *@Controller*.

First, we must enable this feature by setting the *@EnableSpringDataWebSupport* annotation on our *CommentStoreApp* like:

```
@SpringBootApplication
@EnableSpringDataWebSupport
// rest omitted
public class CommentStoreApp {
    // omitted
}
```

Second, in our *@Controller* method, we can now pass a *Pageable* as a method parameter along, and Spring Data's web support will do the mapping for us:

```
@RequestMapping(value = "/comments/{id}/paging")
public Page<Comment> getCommentsPaging(
  @PathVariable(value = "id") String pageId,
  Pageable pageable
) throws IOException {
    return service.list(pageId, pageable);
}
```

In *CommentServiceImpl* we will create the delegate to the actual repository method:

```
@Override
public Page<Comment> list(String pageId, Pageable pageable) throws
IOException {
    return repository.findByPageId(pageId, pageable);
}
```

When we execute the endpoint now, Spring Data will create the *Pageable* with default values, and as a result, we will get the first page with max. 20 comments.

For requesting a different page or size, we can send some query parameters. By default, these are mapped as follows:

* page = page we want to retrieve; default: 0.

* size = items per page; default: 20.

* sort = sorting in the form of property,property(,ASC | DESC), e.g: ?
  sort=lastname,desc
    Multiple parameters supported

In case we want different default values for the page request, we can add the *@Pageab-leDefaults* annotation to the *Pageable* parameter in the controller method and change the values.

Testing using @WebMvcTest

As mentioned before in the testing the *WriteController* section, we are going to implement the tests for the *ReadController* using the *@WebMvcTest* annotation and pure mocking.

Let's start.

Create the *ReadControllerTest* under *src/test/java* in the package *de.codeboje.springbootbook.commentstore.restapi* and add the following annotations to the class:

```
@RunWith(SpringRunner.class)
@WebMvcTest(ReadController.class)
@AutoConfigureMockMvc
@MockBean({SpamDetector.class, CounterService.class})
```

The first tells JUnit to use the SpringRunner, so we have Spring support in the test. It is the same as before. The annotations *@WebMvcTest* and *@AutoConfigureMockMvc* provide us with the mock environment.

Without a parameter *@WebMvcTest*, will add all *@Controlller* to the context. However, we only want it to load the *ReadController*, so we declare that.

@MockBean will mock for us the SpamDetector so it will not instantiate the class. It also mocks the *CounterService* of Spring Boot Actuator which is covered in the HealthCheck and Metrics chapter. When used on the class, it will mock those beans, but we can not work with a mock. For working with the mock in a test, we must inject it and use the annotation there.

Next, we will mock the *CommentService* service as a field (we are going to use it) and inject the *MockMvc* too:

```
public class ReadControllerTest {
    @MockBean
    private CommentService commentService;
```

```
    @Autowired
    private MockMvc mvc;
}
```

Now we can write the test. First, we create a dummy Comment and tell Mockito to return it when someone calls *list* on our *CommentService*:

```
when(
  this.commentService.list(
     anyString()
  )
).thenReturn(
  mockReturn
);
```

When the list method is called on the mock with any given pageId (*anyString()*), it will return a list with our comment.

```
@Test
public void testGetComments() throws Exception {
    Comment model = setupDummyModel();
    List<Comment> mockReturn = new ArrayList<Comment>();
    mockReturn.add(model);

    when(
      this.commentService.list(
        anyString()
      )
    ).thenReturn(
      mockReturn
    );

    this.mvc.perform(
      get("/comments/" + model.getPageId())
    )
     .andExpect(status().is(200))
     .andExpect(
        jsonPath("$[0].id",
               is(model.getId()))
     )
```

```
        .andExpect(
            jsonPath(
              "$[0].creationDate",
              is(SDF.format(
                  model.getCreationDate()
                      .getTime())))
            )
        )
        .andExpect(
          jsonPath(
            "$[0].username",
            is(model.getUsername())
          )
        )
        .andExpect(
          jsonPath(
            "$[0].comment",
            is(model.getComment())
          )
        )
        .andExpect(
            jsonPath(
              "$[0].email_address",
              is(model.getEmailAddress())
          )
        );

    verify(
      this.commentService, times(1)
    ).list( anyString());
  }
```

When we call the *perform* method on the mock, it will run the given request in the mock environment. It behaves similarly to the previous section with the difference we send a GET request.

The *andExpect* method accepts a *ResultMatcher* as a check. These are implemented in the *MockMvcResultMatchers*, like *status()*, *jsonpath()*, *header()* or *content()*. The matchers either have their own convenience methods for checking results, or they use *org.hamcrest.-Matchers*, like *jsonpath()* does. Both the Spring and the Hamcrest matchers are static, and we can use static imports here.

Now, let's look at *jsonpath()*, which is the most interesting one. It provides the possibility to check the JSON response of an endpoint. Internally, it uses the JsonPath lib (https://github.com/json-path/JsonPath).

The first parameter is an expression identifying the node we want to check; think of it as XSL for JSON. With *$* we point to the root of the JSON, followed by a dot as the delimiter and then the name of the property we want to use. like *$.username*. However, we retrieve a list and not a single object, so we can use square brackets and an index to access the element in the list; i.e.- *$[0].username*.

The second parameter is a Hamcrest matcher (*org.hamcrest.Matchers*), and in the example, we use the *is* matcher. *is* checks if our given value equals to the value to check by the matcher.

For verifying the username, we would simply do:

```
.andExpect(
  jsonPath(
    "$[0].username",
    is(model.getUsername())
  )
)
```

When the username of the object at index zero in the JSON response is equal to the username in our test model, the test succeeds.

At the end we check that the *list* method was called once on the mock; *verify* and *times* are part of Mockito.

Hamcrest, Mockito, and JsonPath are standard test helpers, and I added some links on the books resource page to get you started to deepen your knowledge.

Exceptions

When a controller method throws an exception, MVC will return a 500 Internal server error with a stack trace. We do not want that for our *ReadController*. When no comment is found, we want to return a proper 404 - Resource not found.

So, let's override the default behavior and define an exception handler. In the *ReadController* class, add a new method and set the *@ExceptionHandler* on it. Its parameter must be of type *Exception*, here *FileNotFoundException*.

Now when our service or controller throw a *FileNotFoundException* it will be caught by Spring MVC and forwarded to our *ExceptionHandler*. The *ExceptionHandler* now has the full responsibility to handle the error.

In the sample application, we will only log the Exception for debugging and return to the browser with a 404 using the *@ResponseStatus* annotation. However, we are not limited to a simple return value; we could even return a rendered error page or a JSON describing the error.

```
@ExceptionHandler(FileNotFoundException.class)
@ResponseStatus(value = HttpStatus.NOT_FOUND)
public void handle404(Exception ex, Locale locale) {
    LOGGER.debug("Resource not found {}", ex.getMessage());
}
```

However, we do not want to add a handler for each individual exception. We can define a *@ExceptionHandler* for *Exception* which will act as a fallback like:

```
@ExceptionHandler(Exception.class)
public void error(Exception ex, Locale locale) {
    //do what you want
}
```

These handlers can be specified on an individual *@Controller*, in a common base class for our controllers, or globally with a *@ControllerAdvice*, or even deeper in Spring MVC with a *HandlerExceptionResolver*. Most of the time, *@ExceptionHandler* and *@ControllerAdvice* work splendid.

The above examples combined in a *@ControllerAdvice* could look like:

```
@ControllerAdvice
class GlobalControllerExceptionHandler {

    @ExceptionHandler(FileNotFoundException.class)
```

```java
@ResponseStatus(value = HttpStatus.NOT_FOUND)
public void handle404(
  Exception ex,
  Locale locale
) {
    LOGGER.debug(
      "Resource not found {}",
      ex.getMessage()
    );
}

@ExceptionHandler(Exception.class)
public void error(
  Exception ex,
  Locale locale
) {
    //do what you want
}
}
```

Manual Testing With Postman

Postman (https://www.getpostman.com/) is a tool for testing APIs available via the HTTP protocol. It is available as a Chrome extension and a Mac and PC application. It is a free helpful tool which has saved me a few times already.

After installing it, import a new collection and point to the File *SpringBootBook.postman_-collection* in the source code of our application. I pre-made the essential requests.

Creating a Comment

By default, the Spring Boot application listens on port 8080.

The endpoint for creating comments is accessible at */comments* and accepts a post request. We also need to enter all our required fields.

After clicking the send button, it will look like this:

As a result, we receive the ID of our newly created comment.

Receiving Comments

The endpoint for receiving all comments is accessible at *comments/* and requires the ID of a page as a request path variable. We will use the pageId of our previously created comments.

Click the send button, and we will see something like:

Now create a comment with one of our spam words in any field. Then we will retrieve the spam comments by using our endpoint *comments/{id}/spam* which also expects a page ID in the request path.

Deleting a Comment

We are going to use the ID of the spam comment for our delete request. The endpoint is available under _/comment/ and requires a comment ID in the path. Remember, each comment is accessible under its own URL and our API allows interaction. To delete the comment, we must change to an HTTP DELETE and just send the request.

We will get a status code of 200, and the comment is deleted. Verify it by resending one of the list requests from before.

Securing Our Application

In the current state, our application is open to everyone. If one knows the endpoint he can read, update, or delete comments. Even in an intranet, we do not want to do that.

Luckily, Spring Boot also provides an out of the box solution for securing our application. Two simple steps will give us basic authentication on all HTTP endpoints which is enough for services like this one.

First, add the Spring Security Starter to the pom:

```
<dependency>
  <groupId>org.springframework.boot</groupId>
  <artifactId>spring-boot-starter-security</artifactId>
</dependency>
```

This will auto-configure Spring Security to protect our API with basic auth and the default username user and a randomly generated password on each start of the application.

However, we want to set our own username and password. Open the application.properties and add:

```
spring.security.user.name=admin
spring.security.user.password=mypassword
```

This will configure Spring Security to use these as the default credentials.

Start the application and every time we access it now a browser asks for the credentials.

We are not limited to basic authentication and can use the full power of Spring Security including Form based login, token logins or OAuth2. In Spring Boot and Single-Page

Applications (http://codeboje.de/spring-boot-single-page-applications/) I cover four security variation when working with Javascript single-page applications. However, these solutions do work for other types of applications too.

When security is enabled, it will also be used in the tests by default, except when using the mock environment. We could turn HTTP Basic Auth off by adding:

```
security.basic.enabled=false
```

to the application.properties in the src/test/resources folder. security.basic.enabled is deprecated thou and in future releases we might need to provide a *WebSecurityConfigurer* in the tests.

If we use any of the Spring Security features for authorization, we can use their test support by adding:

```
<dependency>
  <groupId>org.springframework.security</groupId>
  <artifactId>spring-security-test</artifactId>
  <scope>test</scope>
</dependency>
```

to our pom. Now we can use all Spring Security Test annotations as we would regularly do.

Disabling CSRF

In earlier versions CSRF - Cross-Site-Request-Forgery - was not activated by default, it is thou with the Spring Boot 2 RELEASE version. It will add a Filter which checks for a CSRF token on each change request. The filter runs before any other.

We do not use it in the sample application, so we are going to disable it by configuring Spring Security accordingly. For that, we must provide a *WebSecurityConfigurer* implementation in the Spring context. As it is an interface and we do not necessarily want to reimplement all methods, we can use the shortcut and extend from the *WebSecurityConfigurerAdapter* like:

```java
@Configuration
public class WebSecurityConfiguration
  extends WebSecurityConfigurerAdapter{

    @Override
    protected void configure(
      HttpSecurity http
    ) throws Exception {
        //disable csrf as we do not need it in the sample
        http.csrf().disable()
        //allow basic auth
        .httpBasic();
    }
}
```

We cover more about CSRF and Security in general in Spring Boot and Single-Page Applications (http://codeboje.de/spring-boot-single-page-applications/).

Advanced: Fine-tuning the JSON

As I mentioned before Spring uses the Jackson library for mapping from object to JSON and vice versa. The center of Jackson is the so called *ObjectMapper*. It provides the core functionality, and we can change the way it serializes and deserializes the JSON.

Spring Boot, or better the auto-configurer by Spring MVC, will automatically create and add a *ObjectMapper* to the context. This one is preconfigured to ignore unknown properties on deserialization (*FAIL_ON_UNKNOWN_PROPERTIES* in Jackson) and also loads various modules like Java 8 Dates support for Jackson if they are available on the classpath. Java 8 Dates are auto configured when we use Spring Boot 2.

For many cases, it is sufficient enough to rely on the preconfigured version. If we need to adjust it, we can either do it by adding some properties to the *application.properties* or by overriding the bean in the Spring Context directly.

Configure Jackson by Properties

Spring Boot makes the Jackson properties available under the prefix *spring.jackson*. For example, two of the most common use cases are:

* Serializing Java Dates and Times as Strings

* Changing the property naming in JSON (from default CamelCase to Underscores)

We can change them as follows:

```
spring.jackson.serialization.write-dates-as-timestamps=false
spring.jackson.property-naming-
strategy=CAMEL_CASE_TO_LOWER_CASE_WITH_UNDERSCORES
```

Listing all properties here is a waste of space, you can always find them in the Spring Boot documentation.

Overriding the ObjectMapper Bean

The second way is to override the *ObjectMapper* in the Spring Context and providing our own instance. To do so, we must declare a bean in the *CommentStoreApp* class of type *ObjectMapper* and use the *@Primary* annotation to mark it as the primary bean for this type.

```
@Bean
@Primary
public ObjectMapper initObjectMapper() {
    ObjectMapper objectMapper = new ObjectMapper();
    objectMapper.setPropertyNamingStrategy(
      PropertyNamingStrategy.SNAKE_CASE
    );
    objectMapper.configure(
      DeserializationFeature.FAIL_ON_UNKNOWN_PROPERTIES,
      false
    );
    objectMapper.registerModule(
      new JavaTimeModule()
    );
    return objectMapper;
}
```

We can either create a subclass or directly create a *ObjectMapper*, like in the method above and configure it the way we need it. However, Spring Boot offers an additional way, and we can inject a Jackson2ObjectMapperBuilder_ in our method and use this builder to configure the *ObjectMapper*. It is the one Spring Boot uses internally, too, and auto detects certain modules like Java 8 Date support.

The example from above would look like:

```
@Bean
@Primary
public ObjectMapper objectMapper(
  Jackson2ObjectMapperBuilder builder
) {
    ObjectMapper objectMapper = builder
            .failOnUnknownProperties(false)
            .propertyNamingStrategy(
              PropertyNamingStrategy.SNAKE_CASE
            )
            .featuresToDisable(
              SerializationFeature.WRITE_DATES_AS_TIMESTAMPS
            )
            .build();
    return objectMapper;
}
```

Hint: If you also develop clients for your APIs you could share a common Object mapper for the server and client side.

Recap

Before we continue, let's review what we have covered and check your understanding with a short quiz.

- How do you configure a Spring MVC Controller for handling form posts?

- What is the difference between the Controller and RestController annotation?

- How can you secure your application with Spring Security?

- How can you declare your own ObjectMapper for JSON transformation?

- How do you define a custom handler for Exceptions?

- What does the ResponseBody annotation do?

- How can you test a Spring MVC controller?

In the next chapter, we are going to take a look at logging.

Logging

An application wouldn't be complete without any logging. In this chapter, we are going to look at logging in Spring Boot.

Spring Boot uses Logback for logging by default. It is also set up to enable routing from common Java logging libraries like Java Util Logging, Commons Logging, Log4J or SLF4J.

In the sample application, we use SLF4J which is a simple facade for logging in Java. We use SLF4J interface for logging and remove a hard dependency to any logging framework in our code. Logback and Log4J can be used with SLF4J.

To obtain a logger instance, we call *getLogger* of the *org.slf4j.LoggerFactory*. The Method is static, and we can create a constant in our class, e.g.- *ReadController*:

```
private static final Logger LOGGER =
  LoggerFactory.getLogger(ReadController.class);
```

Now we can use *info*, *debug*, or any of the other logging methods.

By default, our log message is printed on the console. This is not suitable for running the microservices later, so we are going to change it to file based logging.

Logging to File

Spring Boot offers two properties to enable logging to file. They can work together too.

The properties are set in our *application.properties*.

* logging.file: Specifies a file to write in; it can be a relative or absolute path.

- logging.path: Specifies a directory where to store the log file. If logging.file contains a relative path or just a file name, it will be placed in logging.path. If logging.file is not present, the log file is named spring.log

The file logger is rolling and will create a new file at a size of 1o MB. Previous versions are kept and named by date and the rolling number and is also gzipped.

Changing the Log level

Spring Boot provides a way to modify the log level with properties set in the *application.properties*.

They are prefixed by *logging.level*, followed either by *root* for the root logger or by packages - down to full class. The value is the log level, one of TRACE, DEBUG, INFO, WARN, ERROR, FATAL, OFF.

Setting the root logger to WARN looks like:

```
logging.level.root=WARN
```

When we want to change the logger for the Spring Framework to only report errors:

```
logging.level.org.springframework=ERROR
```

Hint: When you move your microservice into production, make sure not to set the global logger to DEBUG, nor the Spring Framework. It will flood your disk.

Changing the Log Pattern

Along with the other logging configuration, we can also change the log pattern with two simply properties.

First, with *logging.pattern.file* we change the pattern for the file output.

Second, with *logging.pattern.console* we change it accordingly for the console output.

We can use Logbacks log pattern here:

```
logging.pattern.file=%d{HH:mm:ss.SSS} [%thread] %-5level %logger{36}
%X{SBBRequestUUID} - %msg%n

logging.pattern.console=%d{HH:mm:ss.SSS} [%thread] %-5level %logger{36}
%X{SBBRequestUUID} - %msg%n
```

Advanced Logging

Custom Logging

The previous setup works for many cases but sometimes our infrastructure is a bit more complex, and we need to have more control in setting up the logger. Spring Boot has us covered for that as well.

When it detects a configuration file of our logging system, i.e.- *logback.xml* for Logback, it will use that for initialization. However, Spring will not control our logging system now and might not be able to use certain Spring features, e.g.- using Spring profiles in the log configuration.

To enable better Spring integration, it will also look for a configuration file with *-spring* in the name, so *logback-spring.xml* for Logback.

With this variation, we can use the full power of Logback and fine tune the appenders, etc.

I included one in the Commentstore App which sets up a bit more; it also uses custom MDC variables.

Follow Requests in Our Landscape

When we are running a bunch of microservices, it really helps when we can track a specific user action throughout our whole system. The easiest way without relying on any other service is to route some identifier along our system and add it to the logging output.

When a user action enters the system, it gets a unique ID assigned, and the request is logged. Now we only need to pass the UUID of this request along with the system. To make that as transparent as possible we will use the Mapped Diagnostic Context (MDC) of our logging library.

An MDC provides a way to add user specific data to the current thread so the logging system can use these in the log pattern; it has the benefit that we do not need to pass it along with our call hierarchy by ourselves.

Let's implement it for our microservice. The code is in the *logging* module in the books GitHub repository.

The UUID is passed as the *SBBRequestUUID* HTTP header along the system, and a ServletFilter will handle it in our microservice.

Create the **RequestContextLoggingFilter** and implement the *Filter* interface:

```
@Override
public void doFilter(ServletRequest request, ServletResponse response,
FilterChain chain)
throws IOException, ServletException {
    try {
        String requestUUID = ((HttpServletRequest) request)
        .getHeader(SBBLoggingConstants.REQUEST_UUID_HEADER);
        if (StringUtils.isEmpty(requestUUID)) {
            requestUUID = createId();
            LOGGER.info("Got request without {} and assign new {}",
            SBBLoggingConstants.REQUEST_UUID_HEADER, requestUUID);

            MDC.put(SBBLoggingConstants.REQUEST_UUID_HEADER,
            requestUUID);
        }
        else {
```

```
            MDC.put(SBBLoggingConstants.REQUEST_UUID_HEADER,
            requestUUID);
        }

        chain.doFilter(request, response);
    }
    finally {
        MDC.clear();
    }
}
```

The *RequestContextLoggingFilter* will check if our header parameter *SBBRequestUUID* is available, and if so, it will set it as our custom field in the MDC. If no UUID is given, we create a new one.

The property, *SBBRequestUUID,* we set here on the parameter can be used in the log pattern, and Logback will automatically add it to the log output.

For example in logback.xml:

```
<encoder>
    <pattern>%d{yyyy-MM-dd HH:mm:ss.SSS} [%thread] %-5level %logger{36}
%X{SBBRequestUUID} - %msg%n</pattern>
</encoder>
```

Or with the Spring Boot property:

```
logging.pattern.file=%d{HH:mm:ss.SSS} [%thread] %-5level %logger{36}
%X{SBBRequestUUID} - %msg%n
```

To use the filter, we must declare it in our *CommentStoreApp* Spring Boot configuration:

```
@Bean
public Filter initRequestContextLoggingFilter() {
    return new RequestContextLoggingFilter();
}
```

Spring Boot will now add our Filter to the default *DispatcherServlet* and thus runs it for all of our endpoints, and before we even enter the *DispatcherServlet*.

When we run the sample application and send a request with Postman the log entries will look like:

```
08:50:11.366 [http-nio-8080-exec-6] INFO  d.c.s.c.restapi.ReadController num1
- get comments for pageId 0815
08:50:11.380 [http-nio-8080-exec-6] INFO  d.c.s.c.restapi.ReadController num1
- get comments for pageId 0815 - done
```

num1 is the UUID used in a manual test.

If we omit the *SBBRequestUUID* header in Postman, a new UUID will be generated and logged. When we provide the header in Postman, it will be used in the log.

Note: The request logging mechanism is now available as a Spring Boot Starter. You can find it on GitHub (https://github.com/azarai/request-logging-starter) and use it freely in your projects.

Changing the Log Level During Runtime

Since Spring Boot 1.5.1, and by using the Spring Boot Actuator, we can finally change the log level during runtime. How to set up the Actuator is covered in the next chapter; here we are exploring this feature only.

Note: Actuator endpoints are, by default, accessible under */actuator/* in Spring Boot 2. However, we do need to enable the logger endpoint and expose it too. More on that in the next chapter.

Under the *loggers* endpoint, the Spring Boot Actuator provides a view of all configured loggers and their states. The requests we are using are also included in the Postman collection in the source code.

When we make a GET request to *loggers* we will receive a JSON like:

```
{
  "levels": [
    "OFF",
    "ERROR",
    "WARN",
    "INFO",
```

```
      "DEBUG",
      "TRACE"
  ],
  "loggers": {
    "ROOT": {
      "configured_level": "INFO",
      "effective_level": "INFO"
    },
    "de": {
      "configured_level": null,
      "effective_level": "INFO"
    },
}
```

First, we get a list of all supported log levels and second, each logger with its current log level.

To change the level of a logger now, we must make a POST Request to the particular Logger with a JSON containing the new log level.

Let's modify the ROOT Logger by POSTing the following JSON to the logger's endpoint *loggers/ROOT*.

```
{
    "configuredLevel": "DEBUG"
}
```

In the console log output, Spring is now generating much noise with all its DEBUG messages. To change it back, just post:

```
{
    "configuredLevel": "INFO"
}
```

HINT: When hunting down bugs in a production environment, start with changing the most specific loggers you have configured and from that go up to more generic ones. Changing the ROOT logger or the logger of the major frameworks to DEBUG, or even TRACE will flood your disk faster than you can change it back.

Recap

Before we continue, let's review what we have covered and check your understanding with a short quiz.

- Can you only use SLF4J for logging?

- Where and how do I configure Logging to a file?

- How do I change the log level?

- Can you customize the logging in Spring Boot beyond the previous questions?

- What problem solves the "Follow Requests in your Landscape" section?

In the next chapter, we are going to take a look at metrics and health checks.

HealthCheck and Metrics

Spring Boot includes several features to help us monitor and manage our application when it is in production. We can manage and monitor our application using HTTP endpoints or JMX. The HTTP endpoints are only available with a Spring MVC-based application like ours.

These production-ready features are called Actuators.

To enable the functionality, add the Actuator Starter to our comment store pom:

```
<dependencies>
  <dependency>
    <groupId>org.springframework.boot</groupId>
    <artifactId>spring-boot-starter-actuator</artifactId>
  </dependency>
</dependencies>
```

The endpoints are configured automatically, and with sensitive defaults, i.e., the shutdown endpoint is disabled, and the only exposed endpoints are health and info.

The actuator endpoints are provided under the path */actuator/* since Spring Boot 2. However, we can change the path by setting the property *management.server.servlet.context-path* in the *application.properties*. It is also a good practice to publish the actuators under a different path than the default one; hackers love unchanged defaults.

Remember to add */actuator/* as the prefix to the paths below.

By enabling this feature, we get multiple out of the box functionality like:

- health checks (*/health*)

- metrics like Tomcat stats, requests per endpoint per HTTP status (*/metrics*)

- multipurpose information (*/info*)

- current environment variables (*/env_*)

- taking heap dumps (*/heapdump*)

- current logging plus changing log levels (*/loggers*)

- and more

In the last chapter, we already used the endpoint for changing log levels. In this chapter, we will cover the two most valuable endpoints when starting out - health checks and metrics.

Sensitive Data and Security

Actuators can contain sensitive data like the health checks, and thus Spring Boot offers ways to control this.

First, all actuators, except health and info, are not, exposed via web anymore in the default configuration. We must explicitly include them. They are, however, still exposed by default over JMX.

We can do so by simply setting the *management.endpoints.web.exposure.include* property in *application.properties* like:

```
management.endpoints.web.exposure.include=metrics,health,loggers
```

This example will allow web access for *health, metrics* and *loggers*. All others are denied, regardless if enabled or not.

Second, as opposed to previous Spring Boot versions, the actuator endpoints are now protected by the same Spring Security configuration as the rest of the application. If we did not provide a *WebSecurityConfigurerAdapter*, it will also use a default configuration which will protect the actuator endpoints. However, if we provide one, we are in charge of protecting the actuator endpoints too.

We did define one for disabling CORS in a previous step, so our actuator endpoints are unprotected right now.

Health Check

This endpoint provides information about the health status of the application. It is often used by monitoring software to check if the system is still operating and notifies when the system goes down or unresponsive.

The kind of information depends on the project. In general, Spring Boot checks the application context for all instances of a *HealthIndicator* and makes them available to this endpoint. Common checks like disk space or the status of database connections are added automatically when a starter is used (or a starter provides it). If something is not covered by Spring Boot, we can always implement our own *HealthIndicator*, and it will show up.

If any of the checks are down, the overall status will be down.

We can access it via HTTP with the */health* endpoint, and we will receive a JSON like:

```
{
    "status": "UP"
}
```

By default, all details of the health check are hidden. We can change that by changing the property *management.endpoint.health.show-details*.

```
management.endpoint.health.show-details=always
```

It accepts the values *always, never,* and *when-authorized*. When using *when-authorized*, we can declare a role with *management.endpoint.health.roles* to restrict health details to particular users. It is, by default, empty and thus allows all authenticated users.

After setting it to always the response will look like:

```
{
    "status": "UP",
    "diskSpace": {
        "status": "UP",
        "total": 120007426048,
```

```
            "free": 31533109248,
            "threshold": 10485760
        },
        "db": {
            "status": "UP",
            "database": "H2",
            "hello": 1
        }
    }
}
```

Metrics

Metrics give insight into various statistics of our application, like how much memory does the application run with, how much is free, how the heap size is used, how many threads are running, and so on. Each starter in the Spring Boot world might add its own metrics to the list. For example, the stats about the data source are only present when a database was detected and configured.

When using Spring MVC, all implemented endpoints are automatically added to the metrics as counters. They will also be grouped by the returning HTTP status codes.

The metrics endpoint is, by default, enabled. However, it is only exposed via JMX by default. For viewing the metrics in the browser, we must list it in the *management .end-points.web.exposure.include* property like:

```
management.endpoints.web.exposure.include=metrics,health,loggers
```

We can access it via HTTP with the /metrics endpoint, and we will receive a JSON like:

```
{
    "names": [
        "jvm.buffer.memory.used",
        "jvm.memory.used",
        "jvm.gc.memory.allocated",
        "jvm.memory.committed",
        "jdbc.connections.min",
```

```
"tomcat.sessions.created",
"tomcat.sessions.expired",
"tomcat.global.request.max",
"tomcat.global.error",
"jvm.gc.max.data.size",
"logback.events",
"system.cpu.count",
"jvm.memory.max",
"jdbc.connections.active",
"jvm.buffer.total.capacity",
"jvm.buffer.count",
"process.files.max",
"jvm.threads.daemon",
"process.start.time",
"hikaricp.connections.active",
"hikaricp.connections",
"hikaricp.connections.creation.percentile",
"tomcat.global.sent",
"tomcat.sessions.active.max",
"tomcat.threads.config.max",
"hikaricp.connections.usage",
"jvm.gc.live.data.size",
"http.server.requests",
"process.files.open",
"hikaricp.connections.acquire",
"process.cpu.usage",
"tomcat.servlet.request",
"process.uptime",
"hikaricp.connections.idle",
"hikaricp.connections.pending",
"tomcat.global.received",
"system.load.average.1m",
"tomcat.cache.hit",
"hikaricp.connections.acquire.percentile",
"jvm.gc.pause",
"hikaricp.connections.usage.percentile",
"tomcat.servlet.error",
"tomcat.servlet.request.max",
"jdbc.connections.max",
"tomcat.cache.access",
"tomcat.threads.busy",
"tomcat.sessions.active.current",
"system.cpu.usage",
```

```
            "jvm.threads.live",
            "jvm.classes.loaded",
            "jvm.classes.unloaded",
            "jvm.threads.peak",
            "tomcat.threads.current",
            "hikaricp.connections.creation",
            "tomcat.global.request",
            "jvm.gc.memory.promoted",
            "tomcat.sessions.rejected",
            "tomcat.sessions.alive.max",
            "hikaricp.connections.timeout"
        ]
    }
```

It gives us a list of all available metrics. To see the actual values, we make a GET to like /
metrics/http.server.requests and receive a JSON with the values like:

```
{
    "name": "http.server.requests",
    "measurements": [
        {
            "statistic": "COUNT",
            "value": 11
        },
        {
            "statistic": "TOTAL_TIME",
            "value": 0.396911299
        },
        {
            "statistic": "MAX",
            "value": 0.034764265
        }
    ],
    "availableTags": [
        {
            "tag": "exception",
            "values": [
                "None",
                "IllegalArgumentException"
            ]
        },
        {
```

```
            "tag": "method",
            "values": [
                "GET"
            ]
        },
        {
            "tag": "uri",
            "values": [
                "/actuator/metrics/{requiredMetricName}",
                "NOT_FOUND",
                "/actuator/metrics"
            ]
        },
        {
            "tag": "status",
            "values": [
                "404",
                "500",
                "200"
            ]
        }
    ]
}
```

We can even drill down by tags by appending a tag parameter in the request. The parameter value is in the form *KEY:VALUE* like:

```
/metrics/http.server.requests?tag=status:201
```

It will only give us metrics for HTTP requests with a status code of 201 (Created). Multiple tag parameters are supported.

As with the health checks we can, of course, add our own metrics with using the Micrometer MeterRegistry.

Implementing a Custom Counter

Spring Boot 2 uses the Micrometer library for metrics. Micrometer is a facade over the most popular monitoring systems. It also provides a way to define custom metrics, like a counter, in a vendor-neutral way.

To create our own counter we need to inject the *MeterRegistry* in our bean and use the counter method to obtain the counter. On the received counter instance, we can use the increment and decrement methods to change the counter value. The counter lives as long as the Spring context.

Let's count in *ReadController*. Inject the *MeterRegistry* like:

```
@Autowired
private MeterRegistry meterRegistry;
```

In the *getComments* method, we will increment the counter every time the method runs:

```
meterRegistry.counter("commentstore.list_comments").increment();
```

The first parameter of counter is the name of our counter and mandatory. Tags are optional and help to drill down metrics later in the monitoring system; as seen in the metrics example in the previous section.

When our counter *commentstore.list_comments* has a value, it is also returned in the metrics request. We can see the counter value under */actuator/metrics/commentstore.list_-comments*.

Recap

Before we continue, let's review what we have covered and check your understanding with a short quiz.

- How do you enable the production ready features of Spring Boot?

- Can you secure the endpoints?

- How do you access the health checks?

- Which Spring Bean do you need to use for your own metrics counter?

- Where can you request your metric?

In the next chapter, we are going to take a look at deploying the application.

Deployment of Our Microservice

In the previous chapters, we have built our microservice and enhanced it with production ready features like metrics and health checks. What remains is the actual deployment of our application. For that, we have a couple of options:

1. Standalone plain Java application - One single Jar (FatJar)

2. Standalone executable on Unix - as 1 but with shell script included

3. Deployment as a WAR file

4. Cloud, i.e.- Heroku, Cloud Foundry

Remember, in its bare essence it is a simple Java application. In this book, we will cover the most used version and deploy our application to a Unix system (Option 1 and 2). However, I offer tutorials for cloud deployment on the Spring Boot School (http://springbootschool.com) page.

Build a Standalone FatJar

This is the simplest deployment variant, as we do not have to set up anything at all. By using the Spring Boot Maven Parent, we already get a configured version of the Spring Boot Maven Plugin. So, whenever we run *mvn package* or *mvn install*, Spring Boot will build a single FatJar file with all the dependencies included. It's in the *target* folder.

Start it with:

```
java -jar comment-store-1.0.0-SNAPSHOT.jar
```

It will start the application as during implementation with the difference, now that everything is included in this single file.

Build an Executable FatJar

Creating an executable FatJar is almost as simple as the previous version. We must configure the Spring Boot Maven Plugin, so add the following plugin configuration into our comment store pom:

```
<plugin>
  <groupId>org.springframework.boot</groupId>
  <artifactId>spring-boot-maven-plugin</artifactId>
  <configuration>
    <executable>true</executable>
  </configuration>
</plugin>
```

This will override the configuration from the Spring Boot parent. The magic property is *executable*.

Next time we run *mvn package* or *mvn install*, Spring Boot will build a single JAR file with all the dependencies and wrap it with a shell script, so it runs as an executable on Unix systems. It is named *comment-store-1.0.0-SNAPSHOT.jar* and is in the *target* directory.

When deploying our application later, we probably may not want the version in the filename or perhaps we may have an entirely different one. We can change it by adding the *fileName* property to the configuration:

```
<plugin>
  <groupId>org.springframework.boot</groupId>
  <artifactId>spring-boot-maven-plugin</artifactId>
  <configuration>
    <executable>true</executable>
    <finalName>sbb-comment-app</finalName>
  </configuration>
</plugin>
```

Building the package now, the Spring Boot Maven Plugin will name our file *sbb-comment-app.jar*.

The generated app works out of the box with init.d or systemd and accepts *start, stop, restart*, and *status* commands.

For example, copy the application to */var/sbb-comment-app* on a server. Create a symbolic link in *init.d* for the application:

```
sudo ln -s /var/sbb-comment-app/sbb-comment-app.jar /etc/init.d/sbb-comment-app
```

Start the application by executing:

```
service sbb-comment-app start
```

Voila!

If it does not start check the log files and if you have not overridden the location, the log-file is found in */var/log/<appname>.log*.

Of course, do not forget to secure access to the files and folders when going into production.

We can customize the default script in a certain way, i.e.- setting the JAVA_OPTS. For that, we place the options in a configuration file alongside our jar file. It must use the same application name as our jar file and have *conf* as the file extension:

```
JAVA_OPTS=-Xmx1024M
LOG_FOLDER=/custom/log/folder
```

Advanced: Use An Own Launch Script for the Unix Executable

Sometimes, a use case is not covered by the default start script, so we have to declare our own.

We can declare our own starter script by adding the property *embeddedLaunchScript* to the Spring Boot plugin configuration in our pom and specify the name of the launch script. The script is a regular shell script which should run on the target server platform. Now, it is the sole responsibility of this script to launch the application.

Recap

Let's review what we have covered and check your understanding with a short quiz.

*   Does Spring Boot create a Unix executable of your application by default?

*   Can you start a Spring Boot application as a simple Java program?

*   Can the Unix executable be used with init.d?

*   How can you define properties, like JAVA_OPTS for your application?

*   How can you define your own start script when deploying as a Unix executable?

Where to Move Forward?

You have built your first microservice with Spring Boot now.

Congratulations!

Now, go and build a second one. And a third one. And a fourth one.

Stick with a simple CRUD API and practice it.

You will notice that at the fourth time you implement one, you will be much faster and didn't have to think as much anymore how to do it. You just did it.

Do as many rounds as you need until you feel comfortable enough implementing a basic CRUD API without thinking much. And then move on to the next topic you want to expand your knowledge in, e.g., querying MongoDB with Spring Data, or different ways of securing your API with Spring Security.

As a starting point, you can use the resource page (http://codeboje.de/sbb-resources) of this book. In it, I collected the links from the book for your convenience and also link to the Spring Boot School containing more tutorials (free), as well as some other books to move you forward.

These books cover the security aspects of your Spring Boot API when working with single-page application and standard microservice strategies and patterns for making your microservice more reliable with using the power of Spring Cloud and Netflix OSS.

If you have further questions, or want advice on how to continue, do not hesitate to reach out. I am glad to help. You can either reach me via my site codeboje.de, or directly via my exclusive email at book@codeboje.de.

I hope you've enjoyed my book and that it has helped you.

Happy coding,

Jens

Appendix A: Brief Introduction to Maven

Maven is a build automation and dependency management tool used primarily for Java projects. It addresses two aspects of building software: First, it describes how software is built, and second, it describes the dependencies.

Maven projects are configured using a Project Object Model (pom), which is stored in a *pom.xml* file. The pom is written in XML.

You can download it at the Maven project site (https://maven.apache.org/download.html) and install it following the installation tutorial (https://maven.apache.org/download.html#Installation). Alternatively, you can get it with the package manager of your choice. If you are using Eclipse or the Spring Tool Suite, it is already included and can be executed inside the IDE. However, if you want to run it on the command line, you must install a regular version.

It requires only Java to be installed and is a command line tool.

The Project Object Model

Now, let's start with an overview of the pom and then move to where to put your files and how to compile.

For the spam checker from the first chapter, the pom looks like:

```
<project
  xmlns="http://maven.apache.org/POM/4.0.0"
  xmlns:xsi="http://www.w3.org/2001/XMLSchema-instance"
  xsi:schemaLocation="http://maven.apache.org/POM/4.0.0
    http://maven.apache.org/xsd/maven-4.0.0.xsd">
  <modelVersion>4.0.0</modelVersion>
```

```
    <groupId>de.codeboje.springbootbook</groupId>
    <artifactId>spring-core-start</artifactId>
    <version>0.0.1-SNAPSHOT</version>

    <properties>
      <maven.compiler.source>1.8</maven.compiler.source>
      <maven.compiler.target>1.8</maven.compiler.target>
    </properties>

    <dependencies>
      <dependency>
        <groupId>org.springframework</groupId>
        <artifactId>spring-context</artifactId>
        <version>4.3.10.RELEASE</version>
      </dependency>
    </dependencies>
  </project>
```

The project tag declares the project structure and always contains a modelVersion which defines the pom version. They are fixed for us, so leave them as is.

Each project is identified by three values:

* groupId

* artifactId

* version

Maven uses these to locate the correct version of a module. Versions can either be a release or a snapshot. A Snapshot is a working version and is identified by ending the version with -*SNAPSHOT*. The difference is that you can update a snapshot version in a Maven repository but not a released one. A release is fixed and makes sure that you can build the exact same artifact for this particular version.

The next thing is, we set some properties like to explicitly use Java 8 as it usually falls back to Java 1.5.

Under the dependencies section, we can declare the dependencies of our project. These are also identified by groupId, artifactId and version.

Where to Put Your Classes

Maven assumes a rather strict way of how to layout your project. However, it does have its advantages.

- src/main/java: the place to put your Java packages and source files

- src/main/resource: non-source code resource files which should be included in the resulting artifact like the application.properites in Spring Boot

- src/test/java: the Java tests

- src/test/resources: non-source code resource files for the tests

The folders are relative to your pom file.

How to Build

Open a terminal in the directory where your pom is.

The command line application is *mvn*.

To build the source code use:

```
mvn clean install
```

This will, first clean the output directory *target* and then compile your application and run all tests. If the test pass, it will bundle it into a Jar file and place it under *target*. If tests fail, it will complain about it on the console and point you to the failing tests.

Multi Module Projects

Usually, a Maven project is a single module and artifact. However, when working in multiple modules, you had to manually install each of them each time you change something or make a release. To make it a bit easier, you can group those modules into a so called Multi Module Project.

This project type has a pom at its root. However, this pom only defines a set of modules. Each of those modules exists in its own sub-directory and with its own pom.

When you build now in the root project, it will build all the sub-modules at once; thus reducing the amount of "clean installs".

I used such a module for the comment store in the GitHub repository. It also contains the build instructions.

Move Your Microservice to the Next Level

In this pocket guide, you will learn how to make your Spring Boot microservice infrastructure resilient by using Spring Cloud and Netflix OSS.

http://codeboje.de/spring-boot-intermediate-microservices/

Integrate it With a
Single-Page Application

Learn 4 ways to integrate your Spring Boot application with a single-page application securely in the same actionable and hands-on approach.

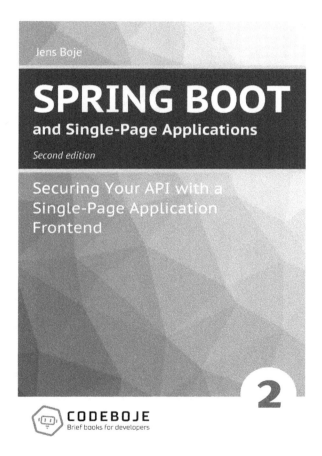

http://codeboje.de/spring-boot-single-page-applications/

www.ingramcontent.com/pod-product-compliance
Lightning Source LLC
Chambersburg PA
CBHW060200060326
40690CB00018B/4182